THE
EXCLAMATION

THE
EXCLAMATION

The Wise Choice of a Spouse for
Catholic Marriage

Patricia A. Wrona

ISBN: Hardcover   1-4134-6936-1
         Softcover   1-4134-6935-3

Nihil Obstat
Reverend William H. Woestman, O.M.I., J.C.D.
Censor Deputatus
July 28, 2004

Imprimatur
Most Reverend Edwin M. Conway, D.D.
Vicar General, Archdiocese of Chicago
August 2, 2004

The *nihil obstat* and *imprimatur* are official declarations that a book is free of doctrinal and moral error. No implication is contained therein that those who have granted the *nihil obstat* or *imprimatur* agree with the content, opinions or statements expressed in the work, nor do they assume any legal responsibility associated with its publication.

Unless otherwise noted, Scripture verses are from the Catholic Edition of the Revised Standard Version of the Bible, copyright © 1965, 1966 by the Division of Christian Education of the National Council of the Churches of Christ in the United States of America. Used by permission. All rights reserved.

Excerpts from the English translation of the Catechism of the Catholic Church for use in the United States of America, Copyright © 1994, United States Catholic Conference, Inc.—Libreria Editrice Vaticana. Used with permission.

This book was printed in the United States of America.

To order additional copies of this book, contact:
Xlibris Corporation
1-888-795-4274
www.Xlibris.com
Orders@Xlibris.com
26160

CONTENTS

Acknowledgments

I dedicate this book to Pat, and by doing so, hope to acknowledge the contribution he has made to my life. Without him, I would have little understanding of the process of discerning the will of God, particularly in the context of the call to the vocation of marriage. I thank Pat too for distilling this process down to the shorthand expression "the exclamation," which so aptly describes the joyful knowingness that the discernment of marriage must lead to, and therefore simply had to be the title. (Leave it to you to "bottom line" something so incredibly well.) I love you.

I also acknowledge the other men I met along the path who, each in his own way, pointed me to the vocation of marriage: Joseph, Craig, Mark, Mark, Pat . . . you are each still dear to me for what you brought into my life and for your unique contributions to my journey.

I know I would not have been able to write any of this without the following people's love and support:

To my mother, who taught me that love endures all things, and is stronger than death.

To my father, whose passion lives on in me, and my sister Pam, whose creativity and drive inspire me still.

To my sister Bev and her husband Jay, whose marriage has always been an example to me, and my nephews Michael and Paul, who bring me so much joy.

To my friend Sue, whose camaraderie on the difficult road of seeking a godly spouse was oftentimes the only thing that kept me going. Love you, my friend.

To my dear Judy, who has been there for me through everything, every spiritual trial. You are my angel always.

To my spiritual director, Father John—your scholarship, patience, and priesthood have been a great blessing to me.

To my great friend Cindy, for your courageous example in your own struggles, and your unwavering affirmation that I always follow my heart.

To Erin and "Kam" (Kathy), for all your wit and laughter.

To my many other friends, who endured countless hours of my musings, bending their ears with the concepts, theories, and ideas that I didn't know would eventually find their way into this book, thanks for listening.

To my publisher, Anthony, thank you for believing in the message, and my editor, Steve, for your patience and attention to detail.

I consider it an honor to have written a book for the Catholic men and women everywhere who are earnestly looking for the spouse that God has prepared for you. I pray for you in your journey as you seek the person of your dreams and your heart's desire. Rest assured that the Lord knows exactly what He is doing: "For I know the plans I have for you, says the LORD, plans for welfare and not for evil, to give you a future and a hope" (Jeremiah 29:11).

Patricia A. Wrona
July 2004

Introduction

What This Book Is, What It Is Not, and Whom It Might Help

This book was born out of the frustration of many single, devout, seeking Catholics whom I have run into along my own path to the discernment of the vocation of marriage. Over and over again, I hear single Catholics express their dismay about how little guidance is available on making the most important decision you will ever be called upon to make. If you are called to the married state of life, the selection of your spouse is the greatest choice you are given by the Lord. It is the ultimate exercise of the gift of free will, which God has placed in you. Given the gravity of such a decision, and the dire consequences when a person gets it wrong, one would think that there would be abundant assistance and help available in Catholic literature. Despite this great need, my experience, and that of many other single Catholics, has been that there is really very little in the way of help books to guide us on this important journey.

If you go to any Catholic bookstore, you will find books and manuals intended for engaged couples, newly married couples, or couples experiencing difficulties at the various stages of marriage. There are also books on planning your Catholic wedding, covering topics such as what hymns to use or Scripture readings to select. There are books on divorce, remarriage and annulment, and how to navigate through those difficult waters. Lacking, however, is a guide for the single Catholic who has not yet come to the decision to become engaged but who is truly seeking to know God's will for his or her life concerning the vocation of marriage and the proper discernment of the people they are dating.

Of course, there are many, many secular books and magazine articles about the oftentimes frustrating search to find a good man or woman to marry. The secular bookstores are full of titles on how to find the "love of your life," how to meet the man of your dreams in thirty days or less, or how to make someone fall in love with you. Such secular books may have a place in your Catholic marital journey. There is wisdom to be found in the secular world about finding a person who is compatible with you, with whom you might have a better chance of marital success "in the world," perhaps. God has given us the social sciences, like psychology, and those disciplines can enlighten us in some aspects of choosing a spouse, whatever our religious faith.

While there are many books that might guide you on how the world would think you should select your mate, what has been lacking is a book to help a person of faith, and in particular, the Catholic faith, decide whom to marry. As you select the people you allow into your life, as you get more serious with someone, but are not yet at the point of a marriage proposal, that is where the guidance is sparse and the need is great.

Why is help so necessary at these earlier stages? Can't you just wait and figure out if someone is God's chosen spouse for you after you get engaged? Isn't that what engagement is for? Yes, to some extent, and a broken engagement is better than a divorce later on, to be sure. But why let it come to that? Discernment of whether someone is God's chosen spouse for you can come much earlier, and frankly should, to spare the hearts, feelings, and time of everyone involved. The reason we need help in this process early on is that it is in the early stages of dating that you might pass up someone who really is the right person for you. It is in dating that you might waste a great deal of time and energy and squander opportunities by dating someone who is never going to be the right person for you, who never was God's chosen one for you. Even worse, you might end up engaged and then married to someone who is not right for you, who is not the right helpmate that God had in mind, because you let it go too far when you could have discerned better early on. It is so easy to make a mistake in this critical period. There needs to be more guidance in discerning a Catholic spouse, and it is hoped this book can provide some of that help.

In an ideal world, you would be surrounded by devout Catholic family members, with successful marriages of their own, to whom you could go for advice and counsel, and who would have all the time in the world to sit with you and discuss your love life. Or that there would be a priest available for every one of us to talk to, who had sufficient time to advise each of us on the ups and downs with our latest boyfriend or girlfriend, and what it all means to our call to the vocation of marriage. But this is often just not the case in most families and parishes. While you would hope for more assistance from your faith community, you might well find yourself on your own on this journey, for the most part.

Perhaps this is just the way it should be. As you are discerning the movements of God's will upon your heart concerning marriage, you and only you can decide what you are called to do. Spiritual advisors, devout friends, and loving family can give their input, but the selection of your spouse is absolutely up to you. No one can decide this for you. As this decision is highly personal and subjective, in making such a decision you might feel very alone. This book is meant to be a trustworthy companion on what might seem like an uncertain, at times even lonely path.

You need to arm yourself with as much help as you can get, because discernment of your spouse is the most important thing you will do in your call to the vocation of marriage. Get that part of the decision right—get the "who" right—and you will have a much better chance of happiness and true fulfillment in your calling.

This book is not meant to displace the work that an engaged couple will do through an "Engaged Encounter" weekend or Pre-Cana class. Those parish- or diocesan-sponsored (and often required) exercises are efficacious and very enlightening to any couple that goes through them with open hearts, open eyes, and open ears. This book might still be helpful to a couple who is already engaged, as a reality check that they have really done everything they can to make the right and proper decision about their call to the vocation together.

While the materials and exercises that an "Engaged Encounter" or Pre-Cana class uses might also be helpful to the searching Catholic single who is not yet engaged, this book is particularly directed to someone looking for or in a "pre-engagement" relationship, in which the parties are seeking, trying, and actively discerning whether they are right for each other. While discernment continues even in the engagement period (Now that we have made our intentions public, are we really doing the right thing? Are we really called together?), right up to the "I dos," engagement is largely a period of confirmation, to see if your discernment was in fact correct, that this person to whom you are now engaged really is meant to be your spouse. This book is addressed most directly to the Catholic single who is trying to find the answer to that question in the first instance.

This book is not about how to find a man or a woman with whom to have a romantic relationship. How to pick up date at a bar, or in class, or at the supermarket are all topics treated in depth in the secular media. This book presupposes that you know how to find viable candidates for consideration as your Catholic spouse. (Here are two clues: at church or through other Catholics.) This book might give you more ideas on just who actually is a viable candidate to be your spouse, and by that, it might inspire you to identify new places or ways to look for him or her that you might not have thought of before. But this is not a "how-to" book on how to snag a boyfriend or girlfriend. It's assumed you already have one (or a few) in mind.

This book is also not a treatise on divorce, second marriages, or annulment. The most basic premise of this work is that the person you are discerning about, that you have in mind to possibly marry, is a person free to marry in the Catholic Church. If the person you are dating and wondering if they are your spouse sent from God, is *not* free to marry you in the Catholic Church, it could not be more clear: *at present, he or she is not the one for you.* If the impediment to marrying him or her is something that can be cleared up by an annulment, then it is possible that you might be able to discern that they are your heaven-sent spouse at some time in the future, but they are not now that person. God would not send you someone whom you cannot marry in the Church, in the faith that you hold so dear. The Catechism's teaching on marriage and annulment is clear that each party must be available for a sacramental marriage. And that is what you are really seeking: a holy, sacramental marriage.

Who is this book for, then? It is for Catholics who are devout and serious about their faith, particularly as it concerns marriage, children, family, chastity, and morality. If you are a "cafeteria Catholic" who picks and chooses what they want to believe, this is probably not the book for you. This writing presupposes that the reader embraces all the teachings of the Catholic Church and wants a spouse who believes the same things and who has already appreciated the great value of a deeply held, shared faith. This book is for the person who feels that the way the world tells him to look for a spouse is not the way God would have him look. This book is for the person who knows that God's ways are not the world's ways, and that the secular method of selecting a spouse is not going to work for him.

Primarily, this book is written for Catholic singles who are in the various stages of romantic relationships, just meeting each other, starting to date, dating, even seriously dating, in long-term relationships, but are short of actually being engaged. It is for anyone who is trying to make their way through the exhilarating, yet daunting, evaluation of what God wants for their life, and whom He wants in their life, as far as marriage is concerned.

This book is also for young people, just starting out in their dating life, who are firm in their faith and want to make sure that they don't make any serious mistakes in their dating, or waste their college days or early adulthood (probably some of the best times in life to find a spouse) by being involved with someone, or a long string of someones, who are not what God has in mind.

This book is for people who find themselves in the midst of a difficult relationship, struggling to figure out what the problem is, why you have feelings for but can't seem to get to marriage with the person. This book might give you a reality check on the kind of relationship and spouse God has in mind for you, against which you can measure your current relationship.

This book is for people who have suffered the loss of a relationship, through a break-up, a broken engagement, even divorce. By reading this book, you might come to realize where you mis-discerned in that relationship, how you got it wrong that time around, so that you can move forward, armed with a new set of directions and ideals that will help you discern correctly what God's true will for your life is next time around.

This book is also for those who are not even sure they are called to the married vocation. If in reading about this process the depth of self-revelation, brutal honesty, and intimacy that is required in discerning the person with whom you could enter into a sacramental marriage is not a process that excites you, invigorates you, and makes you feel hopeful, then perhaps you are not called to the married vocation at all, but rather are called to another vocation: consecrated religious life, priesthood (if male), or the celibate single life. That is very valuable information for you to know, and know now.

This book can also be an aid to parents of adult children who feel ill-prepared to guide their sons and daughters through this most important decision of their lives. Sometimes it seems that life was simpler in Mom and Dad's era, that it was not so likely you would make a grave mistake in dating or marriage. Many parents are very concerned that their children need sound advice and direction in this area but don't know how to give it or what to suggest, but pray they will be spared a lifetime of heartache. This book might give you some ideas to share with your adult children about how to go about looking for true love in the right way.

Similarly, this book is for priests and spiritual advisors, who are called upon to guide Catholic singles through the difficulties of love relationships and the call to marriage.

If you are in any of these groups, it is hoped that this book will be a valuable tool to you. Love is the only true adventure in life, they say. You are embarking on the thrill-ride of a lifetime, so let's get started discerning the person with whom God wants you to serve Him in the vocation of marriage.

Chapter 1

The Exclamation

People might debate whether God has picked out one special person to be your husband or wife, or if there are lots of people to whom you could be happily married. If you took a survey, you would find the idea that there is a "one and only" love out there for everyone is a pretty widely held ideal. It's such a romantic notion, isn't it, that somewhere out there is a Prince or Princess Charming who is longing and pining away for you, just as you are for them. The movies, love songs, romance novels, and television soap operas all reinforce this idea. But is there a religious basis for this belief, particularly in the Catholic faith?

Marriage is a Catholic sacrament that involves not just you but another person. As a Catholic, you can be baptized, confirmed, partake of Holy Eucharist, and receive the anointing of the sick and the sacrament of reconciliation without anyone else's permission. It's between you and the Church.

But the final two sacraments, marriage and holy orders, are different. They are the two "service" sacraments, and you can't just decide for yourself that you are going to participate in them. To be a priest, the Church has to accept that indeed a man has the calling to the sacrament of holy orders. To be married, a man and a woman agree they are called to each other, and enter into the sacrament of marriage together.

While he might be called to the vocation of the priest-hood, every priest comes to the sacrament by a particular path, either a diocesan seminary or through a priestly or-der. So just as a man is called to a particular order of the priesthood, say the diocesan priesthood, the Franciscans, or the Oblates of Mary Immaculate, as the place where he will best serve God in his priestly vocation, men and women are called to marriage with a particular person that will al-low them to give their best service to God. This is what a "helpmate" is, in the truest sense.

There is biblical evidence for God as matchmaker, and a very exacting matchmaker at that. The Lord God Himself fashioned a particular woman for a particular man: Adam and Eve. By examining that divine "fix-up" between Adam and Eve in the Garden of Eden, we can learn a great deal about what God will do to help you identify your "one and only" love—your spouse—too.

The biblical inspiration for this book, and for encourag-ing you to seek God's perfect will in the discernment of your husband or wife in marriage, can be found in the scrip-tural recounting of the creation of the first woman, Eve. Let's start by reading God's Word about when He "fixed up" Adam with his wife, found in Genesis 2:18-25:

> Then the LORD God said, "It is not good that the man should be alone; I will make him a helper fit for him." So out of the ground the LORD God formed every beast of the field and every bird of the air, and brought them to the man to see what he would call them; and what-ever the man called every living creature, that was its name. The man gave names to all cattle, and to the birds of the air, and to every beast of the field; but *for the man* there was not found a helper *fit for him*. So the LORD God caused a deep sleep to fall upon the man, and while he

slept took one of his ribs and closed up its place with flesh; and the rib which the LORD God had taken from the man he made into a woman *and brought her to the man.* Then the man said, "*This at last is bone of my bones and flesh of my flesh*; she shall be called Woman, because she was taken out of Man." Therefore a man leaves his father and his mother and cleaves to his wife, and they become *one flesh.* And the man and his wife were *both naked*, and were *not ashamed*. (emphasis added)

There's a lot going on in that verse of Scripture, and we need to unpack it to understand how it is that Adam knew that this new creature was *his* woman, *his* wife, and the partner that God wanted for him.

First, God started out observing that it was not good that Adam would be alone. Does that mean that everyone is called to marriage? No, not necessarily. Adam was the first man, and at that point, God had made only creatures that were not like Adam in any way. Adam truly was alone in a way that no other person has ever been alone. Of course, it was not good for him to be so alone. We are not in the same situation as Adam. In our day and age, there is plenty of companionship, family and friends, that Adam didn't have at that point in human history. But this is a good reminder that God has called each of us to fellowship and communion with others, and for many of us, that means the communion of marriage.

In trying to alleviate Adam's loneliness, it's interesting that the Lord first brought a whole parade of animals and creatures to Adam to see what he would call them, to see whether he would recognize them as anything special in relationship to himself. It was almost like a test—God testing Adam to see how good he was at this naming game. God brought birds, reptiles, furry animals, and all manner of creatures to Adam, but Adam saw that they were all different from him in some essential way. Adam gave them names that had no relation to himself because he was able to see that they were not like him in kind. Adam recognized they were not something similar to him in nature. Adam was looking for something or someone who was *like* himself. The test that God set up for Adam was seeing if he could pick out that which was like himself, that he recognized as like himself. And God prepared Adam for that first by presenting many creatures that were not like Adam.

We find that Adam went through all the animals, and he knew that none of them was like him, and none of them was the helper that God had in mind for him. God already had stated the kind of helper or partner He had in mind for Adam: one "fit for him." That's pretty specific, isn't it? Not just any helper, but one fit, or suitable, and not just suitable in general, but suitable for *him*, this particular man, Adam.

God has that in mind for you, too—someone who will be a helper to you, in your particular life, time, and circumstances, and who will be suitable, not just in general, but suitable for you in particular.

You can almost feel Adam's frustration during this long parade of beasts and birds, yet nothing touched him in the core of who he *was*, as being like him, and suitable. You can almost feel the Lord's compassion for him, too. When the Scripture says, "God caused a deep sleep to fall upon the man," it's almost as if God felt sorry for Adam—the poor guy was so exhausted and frustrated from not finding any creature who was like him, like what he was seeking in the core of his being.

Does that sound familiar? Don't you feel that way sometimes? That you are going through a parade of inappropriate dates or suitors, and they might as well be from another animal kingdom because they are so unsuitable for you? Adam experienced that kind of frustration, and God knows your frustration too. He worked it out for Adam, and He can work it out for you, too.

So what did God do for Adam? He actually formed a creature out of Adam himself such that Adam would be able to recognize it as like him, similar to him, suitable for him.

Now, God won't form your spouse out of any physical part of you. But God formed our spirits and he formed our physical bodies, and if He formed the first woman from Adam with it specifically in mind that she would be *his* partner, then He certainly is capable of creating, and is likely to have created, a person appropriate for each of us that He calls to the married vocation.

Once His forming and creation of this helper was completed, what did God do? He *brought* the creature to Adam. God brought Eve. It's as if He were off in a workshop somewhere, working on Eve. But that is what the Scripture says, that He brought her to the man. He didn't set her down in the Garden somewhere and just wait for Adam to stumble onto her. No, He Himself brought her to Adam and placed her before him to see what he would do.

That should give tremendous confidence to each of us who are called to the vocation of marriage—that we don't have to worry about simply stumbling onto the right person for us. God is going to bring them to us. We need to work with the grace and follow His prompting, but if this Genesis verse is any indication, God is going to see to it that the partner He has fashioned for each of us is brought to us somehow. What we do with that opportunity might not be so assured, but we can rest on this verse that God is going to bring the person somehow.

Once God brought the creature to Adam, what happened? You see no hesitation in what Adam did. The verse quoted above uses the words "the man said . . ." But there are other translations that say, "Adam exclaimed . . ." A little different, but the context shows that what Adam said, he said emphatically. Without hesitation, he cried out about what he saw before him.

Think about it. After this menagerie of beasts and birds, Adam saw before him a creature that he recognized, so he couldn't help but "exclaim" what he was seeing and feeling and experiencing about her.

What does that word mean, anyway, to "exclaim"? The dictionary definition is "to utter loudly and vehemently, to declare suddenly, a loud remark or cry, expressing joy or surprise." From the Latin roots, *ex* means "out" and *clamare* means "to call," so to exclaim means "to call out." Adam exclaimed, called out with joy, when he saw Eve.

Adam couldn't even contain himself, because he saw something in Eve that caused such a strong reaction in him that was joyful, excited, and couldn't be contained in some way, that the word used in some translations is that he "exclaimed."

And what did he say in that exclamation? "This at last is bone of my bones and flesh of my flesh." He recognized *himself* in the woman. Finally he had an experience of recognition of who *he* was, and who *she* was in relation to him. And you can tell from his words "at last" that he was frustrated by the parade that came before, and that he was overjoyed with what finally he saw before him.

Even the first man, Adam, had to wait for his wife to come along from God. Kind of makes the wait you have had so far for your spouse seem a little more bearable, doesn't it?

This is the first moment that Adam recognized his own personhood, because truly he saw himself now in relation to something else. Maybe that is an experience you will have—that you will see the reality of who you are, good or bad, when your spouse is presented to you. It will certainly be an eye-opening experience for you as it was for Adam.

The first reference to marriage in the Bible is right here, so because of its primacy in the Scripture, we had better really look at it, since it is marriage that has drawn us into this exploration. Man is called to "cling to his wife." The reference is to a specific wife, *his* wife. Not a wife, or his woman, but "his wife." Sounds like a "one and only," doesn't it? And the reference to the "one flesh" union certainly suggests that this is something you get only one chance to get right.

You could stop examining the verse with that "one flesh" line, but we really shouldn't because the next line gives a great deal of context to the verses that came before: "the man and his wife were both naked, and were not ashamed." Neither one was hiding anything from the other.

After the temptation by Satan and the fall from grace, Adam and Eve clothed themselves, so we know that at this earlier point they were both naked when they were introduced to one another by God. That is both literal (they were wearing no clothing) and figurative (they had nothing to hide from each other, were open and honest with one another).

Part of how Adam recognized Eve as being like him, and from him, was in her physical body. Anyone who says that sexuality has nothing to do with selecting a godly mate is ignoring this reality of how Adam, the first man, recognized his wife. In her body, Adam saw that she was like him physically. Compared to cows or goats, that would not be so hard to see. But in her skin, her face, features, arms and legs, feet and hands, and everything in between, he saw something pretty much like himself—a few differences, to be sure, but yes, this one looks a lot like me, Adam must have thought.

Yet Adam also knew that she was not exactly like him— notice he didn't name her "Man." He knew that was who *he* was, and this was not another man—he knew at least that. Adam could figure that out by looking down at his own body and comparing himself to her. Adam recognized that Eve was like him, and yet not like him, and that was precisely what he had been looking and waiting for. Adam saw that Eve complemented him.

The fact that they were "not ashamed" in their nakedness is important. So often relationships between men and women get so complicated because people are ashamed of being who they really are, or ashamed that who they really are will be discovered by the other, and then it won't work out. Starting out with honesty (a form of nakedness of the soul) and truthfulness about who you are, as Adam and Eve did, is a good way to begin.

So there is a lot going on in this familiar Bible verse, one which we may have heard many times but never really analyzed. Having now examined it, what conclusions can we draw from what happened that day when God "fixed up" Adam with his spouse—his wife—Eve?

1. **God brought Eve to Adam.** And God is going to bring the right spouse to each person that He calls to serve Him in the vocation of marriage. God brought Eve to Adam, and He will bring your wife or husband to you too, if marriage is His will for your life. He didn't leave it up to chance for Adam, and just hope that he would stumble upon Eve around some flowering bush in the Garden of Eden. No, He brought her directly to Adam.

That's pretty encouraging, isn't it? God will see to it that the person who is the fulfillment of your vocation comes into your life as well. God will bring the person in. He will give you the opportunity to meet the person that He thinks will best serve you, and you can best serve, and you two will in turn best serve Him, in the sacrament of marriage. But you must choose what you will do once that person comes into your life. Just as Adam gave his consent to the incredible gift that God brought to him—this woman, his wife, his spouse, who was just right for him—you too will have the responsibility of actually choosing your spouse.

Adam might have had it a little easier than the rest of us. After all, there was only one woman around in Paradise; he didn't have to choose from among several women. Also, at this point Adam was not tainted yet by original sin, so he probably had a clearer head and more open heart than we might have now, given our sinful nature and fallen state. But Adam got to choose his wife when God offered Eve to him, and you too will have the chance to choose your spouse when God brings him or her into your life.

2. **Adam was frustrated by his wait** for a spouse and the loneliness of the process was wearing on him. Adam was so frustrated and exhausted from all that came before that moment, all the naming of the beasts and animals, that he had to be put to sleep for God to do His work. Let's hope it's not as bad as all that for you, but realize that God is at work, and just as with Adam, He is doing something here that makes sense to Him, so who are you to argue? Sit back, relax as Adam did, and let God do His work. He might have work to do on you first. Maybe there are things he needs to take out of you, maybe nothing quite as extreme as a rib, but maybe a bad habit, an attitude, some hurt or pain from a past relationship that needs to be healed in you. Maybe you even know what that is right now. Let God do His work on you.

Or maybe God has some fashioning that He needs to do with your spouse while you wait. Can you even imagine the whittling and molding and shaping that it takes to make a whole woman from a man's rib? While that might be a bit figurative, there could be growing or pruning that your spouse needs to undergo that you don't even know about yet. You will know some day, when you hear her story, what she was going through, how God worked on her and her heart to prepare her for you, but right now, you don't get to know. So trust in Him and let God do His work and when you and your spouse are both ready, He will bring her to you as He brought Eve to Adam, in His perfect time.

3. **Adam recognized Eve** as like himself. Adam had to go through a lot of creatures first who were not right for

him, not fit to be his helpmate. So might you before you recognize a person who is like you. You might go through a long life of dating, full of frustration, as Adam was frustrated and exhausted by the parade of creatures that God presented to him. But as with Adam, God might be testing you to see if you first know yourself so that you can pick out the helper, the mate, that is right for you. Adam was primed to pick out Eve, to get the right answer, because of all that he saw that went before her. So don't despair if it seems there is a long line of all the "wrong" people coming into your life. It all may just be priming for you to be able to recognize the "real deal" when God brings that person to you.

4. **Eve was like Adam** in many essential ways. The male and female bodies, which were what Adam was using as his basis of comparison, are more alike than unalike, and he recognized that in Eve. So too, similarities are going to be the first point of connection for you with your spouse. What those similarities should be for a Catholic marriage to be most successful will be discussed in Chapter 4, but rest assured, they are similarities upon which a solid Catholic marriage is based, and that is definitely something you are going to have to look for when discerning the vocation of marriage. You will be looking for a person who is similar to you, especially in the beliefs and practice of your Catholic faith.

5. **Eve complemented Adam** in the ways in which they were different. We don't know anything about their personalities, but we know that Adam knew Eve in her nakedness, and that her physiology, while the same as his in many ways, was also different in some respects. What he saw too was that she was a complement to his own body.

You are looking for someone who complements you in important ways. You are not looking for someone who is exactly like you in every respect but rather different in some ways, and those differences will complement you, balance you out and complete you somehow, as Eve did for Adam. **6. Adam recognized Eve as his wife in part by her sexuality.** While the verse does not come out and say it, we can infer that Adam was thrilled with Eve, so much so that he exclaimed over her and expressed that "at last" she was with him. He didn't say, "Oh, yes, ahem, this one seems pretty good." He exclaimed when he saw her. Sounds like a pretty strong reaction. As we will see in Chapter 9, the Church teaches, and you need to embrace, that your sexuality and your sexual attraction to your spouse are God-given, holy, and some of God's greatest gifts to our human existence *if* viewed and used in the context in which God meant for them to be expressed; that is, in the covenant, the sacrament, of marriage. There is one person you *should* be sexually attracted to, and that is your spouse. So part of the discernment of your spouse will be in your physical attraction to him or her. That was part of how Adam recognized Eve, and will be for you too, when you discern your spouse.

7. Adam and Eve were totally open with each other, "naked" before each other, when they met, and had no shame about it. There was really nothing to hide; neither one had a past, neither one had other loves or partners before. Maybe it was easier for Adam and Eve than for us, but the lesson is that they were able to see what they needed to in each other, to recognize each other, because of their nakedness, their complete honesty in revealing who and what they were. If you want to properly discern whether someone is your spouse, you will have to approach yourself and that person with the same honesty as Adam and Eve did.

8. Adam had a sense of knowing Eve, really from the first he saw her. He laid eyes on her and he recognized her, he was drawn to her, he felt she was like him, she seemed compatible to him, she comforted him in their likeness, and she complemented him with her differences; he had a physical response to her ("bone of my bones and flesh of my flesh"). For Adam, that knowing happened right away. You too will have this knowing sense that a person is the spouse God has selected for you. It can happen for you right away, as Adam knew instantly. It might be that lightning-bolt sense, like Cupid's arrow in your heart. Or your sense of knowledge may grow slowly and take hold of you over time (remember, we don't have it quite as easy as Adam in the Garden of Eden when it comes to figuring these things out). The thing to remember is that you don't get to decide the timing of how God will unveil the gift of your spouse to you. But at some point you will indeed know, just as Adam knew Eve was the suitable helpmate for him.

So just what is it that we seeking Catholics who feel called to the vocation of marriage—to serve each other and, in turn, serve God as husband and wife in marriage—are really looking for?

"The exclamation."

You are looking for the exclamation—that same exclamation that Adam uttered, that recognition, that joyful knowingness that you have found the person who is to be the spouse that God has fashioned for you and brought to you.

Does "the exclamation" mean you will fall in love at first sight, as it seems Adam did? No, but it might include an experience like that. For someone to be your "exclamation," you will certainly be in love with them, but it does not necessarily include that "love at first sight" experience. Does "the exclamation" mean you will have a sign, a lightning bolt from heaven, when you are with the person? No, it doesn't necessarily include that, though it could. Even if you did think you felt "the exclamation" at first sight, you would need to test it in this process of discernment as you date the person.

What "the exclamation" really means is that at some point you will know, just as Adam knew. The exclamation was not necessarily just a reaction; it was a conclusion that Adam reached. He reached it based on data and evidence, but once he gathered the evidence and processed it, he *knew*. It is hoped that this book will help you find and understand your exclamation when you experience it, and from it recognize the person who is to be your spouse, in that same profound and undeniable way Adam did. The exclamation was not just for Adam. He was the prototypical human, but that experience of knowing that someone is the helpmate, the partner, that God has fashioned and brought to you, can be known by you today just as it was known by Adam in the Garden. God wants nothing less for you and will see to it, but you have do your part, just as Adam did. Like Adam, you are called to discernment of the vocation of marriage. So let's begin the journey to your exclamation, and discerning your holy spouse.

Chapter 2

Am I Even Called to the Married Vocation?

Before you can begin to discern if a particular person is the person with whom you are to share the married vocation, you have to discern in the first instance if you are indeed called to the married vocation in general. Your initial responsibility is to discern what state of life you are called to, and whether you are in fact called to the married vocation.

What is a vocation, anyway? It is being called by God to live a certain state of life. A vocation should instill in us a longing to be who we really are, to reflect what is already in us, and to best use our gifts and capabilities. A vocation should allow you to "be the self that you are, and be that perfectly" (St. Francis de Sales).

What does it mean to discern your vocation? It means that you must determine the source of your feelings, your longings, your inspirations, your gifts, and the spiritual manifestations that are occurring in you and around you for the purpose of deciding if they are a divine calling to a particular way of life: the religious life, marriage, or celibate singlehood. Discerning a vocation should be a joyful recognition in you of your relationship to others (for the priest, the Church; for the married, a spouse; and for the single, the larger Christian community), where you see the fulfillment of your own spirit in seeking the good of the spirit of the other.

Any devout Catholic should first consider the call to the religious life, and then look for feelings, signs, and manifestations that indicate that you are *not* called to be a priest, a religious brother or a nun. If you are a devout Catholic man, the call to the priesthood or monastic life should be something you are open to, and should discern very seriously. For a woman, the call to the religious life as a nun should also be discerned very seriously. If you are a single woman, you should carefully consider if God is calling you to give your life to Him as an avowed religious sister.

The best practice is that you consider the religious life first, early on in life, to give God the "first chance," as it were, at your life. If you discern about a religious vocation and you are not "called," the process will tell you that. Your superiors, teachers, family, your own heart, and ultimately God will tell you if you are not called to be a priest or a nun. If that is the case, you then can move forward, knowing you gave God the first chance with your life. Then you will not doubt that you are called to the married vocation, or the single, celibate vocation. You can move on with no regrets that you somehow were not open to a religious vocation.

If you do not have a religious vocation, don't just assume you are called to the married vocation. The fact that you are reading this book suggests that you think you are called to marriage. But don't assume that you are, whether you are a young adult, well into adulthood, middle-aged, or even older. Don't ever assume anything when it comes to the mystery of God's call on your life.

The great majority of all people do marry. Does that mean you are called to the married vocation? No. While most people do eventually get married, that does not mean that is God's call for *your* life. You have to discern first if that is what God wants for you in general. Only then can you move on to find out with whom He wants you to live out that vocation.

Now, the temptation is to think that you will know if you are called to the vocation of marriage only if and when you find the person with whom you think you can live out that call. It's as if you find the person first, and then you will think, oh yes, this is what God wants me to do with my life.

That is not the way to approach this most important decision in your life. You first have to discern what God wants for you in general and then you will be able to recognize the specifics. A good analogy is this: a woman feels the call to be a nun before she decides what order she is going to apply to, and where she will live out that vocational call. She doesn't think first, oh, I want to be a Dominican, or a Franciscan, or a Little Sister of the Poor, and then decide she wants to be a nun and embraces the concepts of poverty, chastity, and obedience. It's the other way around. First, she feels the call to the religious life and all it will entail, then she discerns the particulars of that life (what religious order).

The call to marriage works the same way. First figure out if you are called to the vocation of marriage, and then, with that clear direction, you will be able to discern the right person with whom you are to live out the vocation.

There are many books and resources available to help you discern your calling and vocation. Such discernment is helpful, too, with marital discernment because there are many similarities between the call to holy orders and to marriage. Any exploration you do on the one topic will aid you in discerning the other. This is because holy orders and marriage are the two sacraments that focus on service. Both require great sacrifice and suffering. Don't be lulled into believing that the religious life is the more difficult and marriage the easier road. Author Christopher West notes that marriage has four rings: the engagement ring, her wedding ring, his wedding ring, and suffer-ring (West, *Good News About Sex and Marriage*, p. 95). There are many crosses to bear, whatever your state of life.

Here are some questions you can ask about the call to the married vocation. Are you drawn to the lifestyle (closeness, intimacy, housekeeping, childrearing, hard work)? Are you self-sacrificing? Family life will require that in abundance. Do you envy married people with their family and children? Can you cope with having lots of people around you, or are you really someone who prefers solitude? Can you subject your will to that of your spouse and children, deferring what you want so that they can have what they need and want? Do you want to marry for the right reasons and not just as a way to get out of your parents' home, have someone to take care of you financially, or to service your sexual desires? Are you fit for married life in temperament and disposition? The reactions you have to questions like these might attune your ear as to whether you are called to the married vocation.

There are a lot of good analogies that can be drawn from the call to a religious vocation and applied to the call to the married vocation. If you are listening, the call to marriage is very similar to the way a man is called to the priesthood. You have a sense of knowing that you belong in that vocation, like a tug at the heart about what you ought to be doing with your time and talent and gifts. You have a feeling that the place you find yourself in now (that is, outside your vocation) is not where you are meant to be. You have aspects of your personality that you see as fitting into and flourishing in that vocation. When you see the vocation being lived out by others (the priest celebrating the Mass, the mother and father shepherding their children), something in you says, wait, I should be doing that.

This is because the call to a vocation is really God pointing out your path to salvation. A priest becomes a priest not because he is holy but that he may become holy. It is his personal path to holiness, to heaven.

That is our goal: to get to heaven. God has already selected for each of us the best path to salvation. That path for you might be the vocation of marriage, but you have to discern if that is the case and then give your "yes," your fiat, to Him in that call. Maybe the way of salvation the Lord has reserved for you is in the complete emptying of self, the entire self-giving, the loving sacrifice, the full surrender of your body, the true honesty, the nakedness, the humility, the transformation that is experienced in the vocation of marriage.

Thomas Merton's book *The Seven Storey Mountain* recounts his own spiritual path that led him to becoming a Trappist monk. Merton talks about what to do when there is a crisis in a vocation, when a man wants to drop out of the seminary. Merton says you must remember that "you do not come to this vocation alone." What he means is that a man does not come to the seminary alone. He brings with him all the souls of those that his vocation will touch along the way, all the souls he would baptize, marry, absolve from their sins, give the last rites, give the Lord's Body and Blood in the Eucharist, feed, counsel, comfort, correct, and instruct. Merton suggests the man doubting his priestly vocation must note well that all of those people, all of those souls, are in essence with him in the seminary, and should he leave the priesthood in this crisis, then know that he is leaving them behind as well. Merton suggests that in heaven someday, when all is revealed, the man only then will know who all those souls were, and what happened to each soul because he did not become a priest—all those whose eternal salvation was affected by the man's decision to say "no" to his vocation. What an awesome responsibility. In the priesthood, you are not called to that vocation alone.

While it might seem right that a priest would have such

a profound responsibility, so, too, do you who are called to the married vocation. You are not called to marriage alone, and that is an awesome responsibility as well. In that call you carry with you the spouse you are meant to have, the children with which you would have been entrusted, and all the generations to come of that family you were called to have, that would have been raised up to the glory of God. You carry with you all the lives of those that would be touched by your marriage and family, and the community at large, the parish, the schools, everyone you would have touched if you had said "yes" to your vocation of marriage and family. Thinking "So what? So I didn't get married, what is the big deal? I was the only one affected by that decision," is simply not true. Always be mindful that you are not called to the married vocation alone.

Discerning if you are even called to the married life should employ the same process we will explore in Chapter 3 on discerning the will of God. What is God's will for my state of life? You can use all the same tools to discern this preliminary question first, and you should do that.

Looking at one of those tools, holy Scripture, you will find that St. Paul has a strong message about being married or remaining single in his first letter to the Corinthians:

> I wish that all were as I myself am. But each has his own special gift from God, one of one kind and one of another. To the unmarried and the widows I say that it is well for them to remain single as I do. But if they cannot exercise self-control, they should marry. For it is better to marry than to be aflame with passion . . . Now concerning the unmarried, I have no command of the Lord, but I give my opinion as one who by the Lord's mercy is trustworthy. I think that in view of the present distress it is well for a person to remain as he is. Are you bound to a

wife? Do not seek to be free. Are you free from a wife? Do not seek marriage. But if you marry, you do not sin, and if a girl marries she does not sin. Yet those who marry will have worldly troubles, and I would spare you that. I mean, brethren, the appointed time has grown very short; from now on, let those who have wives live as though they had none, and those who mourn as though they were not mourning, and those who rejoice as though they were not rejoicing, and those who buy as though they had no goods, and those who deal with the world as though they had no dealings with it. For the form of this world is passing away.

I want you to be free from anxieties. The unmarried man is anxious about the affairs of the Lord, how to please the Lord; but the married man is anxious about worldly affairs, how to please his wife, and his interests are divided. And the unmarried woman or girl is anxious about the affairs of the Lord, how to be holy in body and spirit; but the married woman is anxious about worldly affairs, how to please her husband. I say this for your own benefit, not to lay any restraint upon you, but to promote good order and to secure your undivided devotion to the Lord. (1 Cor. 7:7-9, 25-35)

St. Paul certainly had a point of view on the issue of whether it's better to marry or stay single, didn't he? Some scholars believe that St. Paul was speaking this way because early believers might have thought that the Second Coming was imminent, could happen any day, and therefore St. Paul wanted them all to be ready and unencumbered by such worldly relationships. Whatever the motivation for his point of view, his point rings as true now as it would have in that situation. As St. Paul says, the married are distracted by serving and pleasing their spouses. And for the great majority of us, that is how we are called and that is what we must do.

The most important way to listen to God's call concerning your state of life is by prayer. The discernment of one's vocation is the most elemental decision you will make in your spiritual life. You need all the help you can get. Call upon the Holy Spirit and the communion of saints to help you, to lead you, and to intercede for you, that God will direct you in the way in which you are called to go.

No prayer is more efficacious than the one you say from your own heart, so talk to God about where He is calling you. He will answer you and guide you in the fulfillment of *your* vocation, whatever it may be. Here are some prayer suggestions.

Prayer for My Vocation
(Author unknown)

Dear Heavenly Father, I believe that You are the Way, the Truth and the Life. You alone love me for who I truly am and for what I am able to become. Though I make repeated mistakes, You continually offer me new opportunities to grow every moment of the day.

Your Son lived the Way that I must choose if I'm to be transformed and to fully develop my potential. His way is the only path that leads to true personhood.

Attuned to Your truth, Father, I am capable of leading a wholesome and worthwhile life. The depth of my service to others is dependent on my grasp of Your Truth.

May your Spirit overflow into my life that I may have Your life to the fullest. Give me the strength and the courage to be all that I can be and not to settle for less.

Realizing that my life is a precious gift from You, may I integrate Your Way, Your Truth and Your Life, and make it my own. Amen.

Prayer for My Life's Vocation
(Author unknown)

Loving God, You fill my life with everything I need to be happy. You know how I can best serve You and Your people. Help me to be open to Your working in my life. Help me to place my hand in Yours and give generously of the gifts You have given me. Let me not be faint of heart in responding to You. Let my life be a reflection of Your love for me, and may I share that love with others who come into my life. Amen.

Prayer to St. Joseph to Know My Vocation
(Author unknown)

O Great Saint Joseph, you were completely obedient to the guidance of the Holy Spirit. Obtain for me the grace to know the state of life that God in His providence has chosen for me. Since my happiness on earth, and perhaps even my final happiness in heaven, depends on this choice, let me not be deceived in making it.

Obtain for me the light to know God's will, to carry it out faithfully, and to choose the vocation that will lead me to a happy eternity. Amen.

Chapter 3

Discerning the Will of God in General

There are Catholic books and resources available on the subject of discerning the will of God in general. We are going to draw here on the writings of the great saints, the Catechism of the Catholic Church, and other scholarly works to put together a list of the sources from which you can discern the will of God in your life. First you have to understand the ways in which God manifests His will in your life in general, whether that be about what type of work you should do, where you should live, what state of life you are called to, or what God would have you do in a particular situation. You can then use these tools of discernment to understand what God would have you do in the most important discernment you will ever make. If you are called to the married state of life, then the discernment is about finding the person you are to share with in the vocation of marriage. We will apply what we learn here to the specific situation of discerning the vocation of marriage later on in Chapter 4.

But first, what does the "will of God" even mean? At the outset, we must be clear that it does not mean that God has a "destiny" for you, like a pre-programmed, already decided course that your life is going to run on, no matter what you do, and you just have to "get with the program." The idea that we have a "destiny" and that we have no choice about it is *not* a Christian concept. People use the term "destiny" colloquially, but "destiny" is really a pagan, classical Greek concept that we are fated, required by the gods somehow, to do what they want us to and we have no choice in the matter.

To the contrary, our God (not Zeus) created us with free will (which is not a classical Greek concept). While He has omniscience about what we are going to do with our free will, and He has a will for what He wants each of us to do, He lets us do what *we* choose. God's hand is upon us, but we author the scripts of our lives with our decisions, with our own free will. God did not create humankind so that He could have a bunch of automatons walking around on earth doing only what He wants. No, while He already knows every choice, and every answer, each of us will give Him in every circumstance, He still created us to let us choose: choose God and His ways, or not; a certain profession, or not; a certain place in the world where to live, or not; a certain person to marry, or not. Each of us as His creation is unique and He allows us to shape our own lives, with our own free-will choices.

If God does not have a pre-set "destiny" for you, but rather wants to let you make good choices for yourself, be assured that He is going to lead you in those choices, if you let Him. That's what we mean by God's will. God has a plan that He would have you follow, that is devised for your greatest good—your salvation—if you will follow Him in it. But how is He going to show it to you and allow you the chance to do what He would have you do? What does it mean to "discern God's will"?

God has a plan for what He believes is best for you, how you can best serve Him, best please Him. He knows what is the best way for you to work out your salvation here on earth so that you can be with Him in heaven someday. He has a better perspective on your life than you do, because He sees it all at once, knows the beginning, middle, and end in a way you don't. He sees your life in an "aerial" view, let's call it. Since He has a much better view on the whole of your life, He is always trying to guide you in the way that will be best for you overall, in the long run, that is, for your salvation. God sees things we cannot because we don't have this aerial view. As author Peter Kreeft says, "we see only the underside of the tapestry" (Kreeft, *Discernment*). So God really does want to lead you and guide you, if you will let Him, because He really sees and knows best.

What are you actually doing when you try to discern the will of God? There is a classic Catholic book on discernment, written by Jacques Guillet, S.J., called *Discernment of Spirits*. Guillet says that when you are discerning God's will, looking at the movements in your life and on your heart, what you are really doing is trying to figure out "which of the movements we experience lead to the Lord and to a more perfect service of Him and our brothers, and which deflect us from that goal" (Guillet, p. 9). Discernment is looking for the things that will lead you to God, not away from Him, because His will is always going to be to have you near Him, and for you to be with Him in heaven some day.

Discerning God's will helps you to make good decisions at the many crossroads of your life. But there is a difference between simply needing to make a decision in your life and spiritual discernment. The difference is where your head and heart are at while you do it. Anyone, even an atheist, can make a decision. It is your approach that renders a decision-making process a "discernment." As Father Thomas H. Green aptly sums it up, "discernment is the art of finding God's will in the concrete situations which confront us" (Green, *Weeds Among the Wheat—Discernment: Where Prayer and Action Meet*, p. 57).

Webster's Dictionary defines "discernment" as the "process or faculty of judging." It is from the Latin roots *dis*, meaning "apart," and *cernere*, meaning "to sift." So discernment means "to sift apart." You are sifting out what is from

God from all the other influences that are coming at you in your particular situation.

The word "discernment" itself suggests there is some ambiguity in what God sends to you or allows you to experience. You have to sort it out. The reason for that is not that God is unclear on what His will is, but that we are not capable of seeing it clearly, given our own human limitations and the interferences that bombard us in our human experience. That is what you are sifting through, as a miner pans for gold. There is a lot of sediment to look at, but only some of it glimmers with the true gold, God's true will, for your life.

With discernment, you have to surrender to God the outcome, if what you really want is to do *His* will. You can't be invested in which way things turn out because if you are, then you are fooling yourself that you are seeking God's will in a situation. St. Ignatius, who wrote the ultimate work on discernment in his *Spiritual Exercises*, calls this process "detachment"—detaching oneself from any end except that which leads your soul to God and your salvation (*Spiritual Exercises*, no. 169).

The process of discernment in the first instance requires the collection of information, evidence, and data. That is the "raw material" of discernment (Green, p. 22). Gathering of information comes before discernment proper. Discernment is actually what is done once information is gathered, to be "sifted apart" then in discernment itself.

So how do you go about gathering the data on God's will? If you want God to lead you, you need to know how and where and when to hear His voice and see His movements in your life's situations to collect the evidence that points to His Will.

There is God's general, overall "will" for everyone, which is so well-known that school children can recite the basic principles for all of us: Do good. Avoid evil. Follow the commandments. Do what the Church teaches. Follow the golden rule. Love your neighbor. These things really guide us to live good lives, our best lives, and that is certainly God's will for each of us.

While living in accordance with these rules, we often see God's will for our lives. Sometimes these things alone will tell us what to do in a specific situation. But sometimes we need to understand what God would have us do in a specific situation, such as where to go to college, what house to buy, what profession to pursue, or whom to take as a spouse. To figure out God's specific will in a particular situation, you really need to look much deeper and closer at what God is saying about your specific question or decision. These are the key ways or places or areas you should look to, to discover evidence or information on God's will for your life:

- Holy Scripture
- Church teaching
- Conscience
- Prayer
- Reason
- Circumstances
- Feelings/personal preferences
- Fruits
- Spiritual direction/advice
- Signs

Let's look at each one of these areas to better understand how you use them to discern the will of God.

Holy Scripture. The Bible is God's Word; it is God talking to you, to me, to each one of us. His Word applies to us today as much as it did in the past. If you are looking for God to reveal to you what His will is, the Bible is one of the first places to go, where God will speak to you in His Word.

This can occur when you are just generally reading the Bible and a passage jumps out at you and grabs at your heart. That can be God speaking to you through His Word when you don't even expect it. This can also occur if you go to the Bible actually looking for answers in a certain subject area, such as, "God, what does Your Word say about how I should manage my money?" You can use a Bible concordance to look up all the scriptural references to "money," and learn about God's will for you in that area. You can spend time in meditation on Scripture. This is when you read until you are inspired to stop and reflect on what you have read.

God can also speak to you in the Liturgy of the Word at Mass. Something in the readings at a particular Mass might touch your heart and answer some questions that were burning deep inside you. That can be God speaking to you about His will for your life. God can also answer you in His Word when you ask Him direct questions in prayer, and then He may bring a verse of Scripture to your mind. You can ask God to speak to you about a particular issue, and then just open up your Bible to a random page and see what verse God has for you there, and see if it answers what you are asking.

If you are seeking to find out what God's will is for your life, holy Scripture is an excellent place to start.

Church Teaching. The great treasure of the Catholic Church is that she is vested with the wisdom and the authority to instruct and teach us about what God wants us to do. Whatever your dilemma, it is likely that the Church in its 2000-year history has either answered your question or has articulated principles that will allow you to answer the question on your own in proper accordance with God's will.

Reading the Catechism of the Catholic Church will provide you with much guidance on what God wants you to do in just about any particular situation. In the myriad of choices we face each day of our lives, the Church is there with answers to guide us. As Catholics, we accept that tradition, history, and instruction as coming from the Lord Himself.

One thing you can be assured about is that God's will will never be in contradiction to the teaching of the Church (or holy Scripture, for that matter). That is because God is consistent, in His Word, His teaching, and His will. As Green says, "God is faithful and cannot contradict Himself" (Green, p. 31). So if you have two choices, and one is in accordance with God's Scripture and the Church, and the other is not, then your choice is clear. God's will for you would never be something that is in violation of Scripture or the Church's teaching. "[As] God can never will evil, the alternatives must both be good, or . . . at least indifferent" (Green, p. 81).

Conscience. Your own conscience is another means by which you can know God's will in a particular situation. Conscience is that part of our spirit that God put in us as a means of making good choices, of knowing right from wrong. The glossary of the Catechism defines conscience as "the interior voice of a human being, within whose heart the inner law of God is inscribed." Conscience is what "moves a person at the appropriate moment to do good and to avoid evil."

Your conscience is your sure and constant guide as you make decisions in life. "'In the depth of his own conscience man detects a law which he does not impose on himself, but which holds him to obedience. Always summoning him to love good and avoid evil, the voice of conscience can when necessary speak to his heart more specifically: "Do this, shun that." For man has in his heart a law written by God. To obey it is the very dignity of man; according to it he will be judged.'" (*Veritatis Splendor*, no. 54, quoting from *Gaudium et Spes,* no. 16).

The Holy Father, Pope John Paul II, wrote that "conscience is like God's herald and messenger; it does not command things on its own authority, but commands them as coming from God's authority, like a herald when he pro-

45

claims the edict of a king. That is why conscience has a binding force" (*Veritatis Splendor*, no. 58). "When [man] listens to his conscience . . . man can hear God speaking" (Catechism, para. 1777).

Conscience is not a feeling, it is a knowing, an awareness of the truth. It's what we judge is right based on what we know of the laws of God and the teachings of the Church. Whether experience proves us right or wrong, we are always accountable for all our actions, and "conscience enables [us] to assume *responsibility* for [our] acts . . ." (Catechism, para. 1781).

The Catechism teaches that "man has the right to act in conscience and in freedom so as personally to make moral decisions. 'He must not be forced to act contrary to his conscience. Nor must he be prevented from acting according to his conscience . . .'" (Catechism, para. 1782). The use of one's conscience is the very essence of the gift of free will.

The reliability of your conscience as a means of discerning God's will is influenced by your education in the faith, life experience, and your practice in exercising your conscience. Conscience is something that is developed over time (Catechism, para. 1784). Every person has an obligation to inform his conscience. The conscience will not contradict holy Scripture or the teachings of the Church. Only an educated conscience can help you make good choices.

There are situations that might present themselves that are not directly answered by the Bible or Church teaching specifically. Then it is your conscience that must primarily guide you. God gave us a conscience so that we always have with us an internalized guide to help us to know His will, because some decisions might have to be made quickly, without time for reading, research, and study. That's what your conscience is for: it's able to stop you or prompt you in a situation on short notice if necessary. It's like an internal monitoring system. God can make His will known to you through your conscience about whether something is right or wrong for you, His will or not, at any particular time.

Prayer. Prayer is talking directly with God. What better way to understand God's will than to talk with Him directly? Prayer is an interaction with God. Prayer shows God that you really are seeking Him—seeking to know Him, seeking to follow Him, seeking to have Him be a part of your life. When you pray, God is working on you. You are most open to His insights and His movement on your heart during prayer. So prayer, and the insights and answers you get during and after praying, are very good indicators of what God wants for you and wants you to do. Without prayer, you cannot lead an authentic Christian life. Prayer is essential to making good choices.

Reason. God gave us brains, and we need to use them. Your own human reasoning is an excellent way to understand the will of God. While God's ways are not our ways, and the human mind cannot ever fully comprehend the mind of God, our brains are pretty good at figuring out what is a good or bad thing for us. While our human reasoning can be clouded by deception, a lack of information, or our emotions, when we are being clearheaded about an issue we can turn to our human reason to help us see God's hand moving in our lives. If you could see the whole plan, what God wants of you really does makes sense. He's always consistent, and everything works together when His will is being done. Your reason will let you see the sense of things, when it's God's will.

The problem with human reason, however, is that it is limited, while God's understanding sees a bigger picture. A great example in the Bible is Abraham, who maybe turned out to be the best "discerner" that the Bible ever recorded. Abraham did not have a son until his old age, and he greatly loved his boy, Isaac. God had promised Abraham that his descendants would be many, that he would be the father of a great nation, and Abraham believed that God's promise would be fulfilled (Gen. 18:18). Obviously Abraham's descendants had to come through his son, Isaac.

But then what happened? Abraham hears a voice that tells him to kill, to sacrifice, his only son. That wouldn't make sense if Abraham is to be the father of many descendants. But what does Abraham do? He follows what he is told anyway, because he believes it is the voice of God, that it is God's will, directing him. He took what he discerned to be God's will even though it made no "sense," as it didn't seem in line with what God had previously told him. But Abraham went with it, with great courage (since, of course, he loved Isaac). He learned that God was testing his faithfulness. God sent an angel at the last minute to stop Abraham. Abraham passed the test and Isaac was spared. This is why Abraham is known as our "father in faith."

So while human reason has its place, it may be that reason will be questioned if other movements of God in your life suggest that reason alone is not sufficient in the context of what is occurring.

You also need to be aware that God's will is not necessarily the most complicated or difficult path, and that just because something is harder does not make it God's will. Just because something is difficult does not make it more likely to be God's will, or because something is easier does not make it less likely to be God's will. As Green points out, it's a Lutheran (not Catholic) idea "that what is most unreasonable to human beings is more likely to be God's will, since 'God's foolishness is wiser than human wisdom, and God's weakness is stronger than human strength' (1 Cor. 1:25)" (Green, p. 36). So just because, when looking at it with human reasoning, something seems harder does not mean it's God's will. Sometimes the easiest, simplest thing is God's will.

You can use your human reason to try to work out a problem as part of your discernment. Using hypothetical questions is a way to do that. St. Ignatius suggests three exercises when trying to decide a course of action:

1. What would you advise another person who came to you with the question you are grappling with?
2. Imagine when you lay dying, what would you then have wished you had done in the situation?
3. When you stand before God in your final judgment, what would you have wished you had done? (*Spiritual Exercises*, no. 187).

Those are pretty serious questions, particularly the last two. But they can be enlightening if you think them through with your gift of reason.

So human reason, though it has its limitations, is a helpful tool for gathering data and discerning God's will for you in order to make good choices.

Circumstances. When you are trying to figure out what God would have you do, look around at the circumstances in which you find yourself. Issues and decisions come up at a particular time and in a particular place in your life. Reading the circumstances can be very helpful in discerning what God wants you to do in a specific situation. For example, God might reveal what He would have you do by making the circumstances of a particular choice more easy for you, where all the practical issues of making that choice fall into place. God controls circumstances by His divine providence—He makes things work together for your good. So the surrounding circumstances can be read and God's will can be revealed through them.

Feelings/Personal Preferences. How you feel about a certain situation could also be a way of God revealing His will to you about a particular choice. Maybe you are feeling uneasy or scared about something because what's happening is not what God wants for you. Maybe you have a particular preference for something that you have held all your life because that very preference is going to aid you later in life to make a good choice in line with God's will for you. While feelings and preferences can change and be subject to many outside influences, reading your own feelings can be a way that God reveals His will to you.

Fruits. Every experience of your life generates a sequence of events and feelings and thoughts that the experience sets into motion. That sequence is either positive in nature or negative or, most often, some of both. So the "fruits" of an experience are often both good fruits and bad fruits. You must analyze and discern the fruits in order to know God's will about your situation.

Let's consider an example, that of taking a particular job. Let's say you want to figure out if it's God's will if you should take a job as a lawyer in a large law firm. After you make the decision and you take the job, you feel anxious (that would be a bad fruit). Once you start working there, you have no time to spend with your family (a bad fruit). After working there for six months, you have developed an ulcer from the stress (a bad fruit). But you are making a good salary, have paid off your debts, and are saving for a house (good fruits). And you are learning a lot, and building a reputation as a good lawyer (good fruit). And you are able to contribute more, financially, to your parish (a good fruit).

So was it God's will that you take the job? And is it God's will that you stay in that job? Reading the fruits can be a tricky thing, because most situations have both good and bad fruits, as with this example. But one or the other generally is more prevalent, and if the good fruits are more abundant, then you are probably doing God's will.

"Fruits" is a word that best describes tangible, concrete things that come into our lives. For example, it would be a good fruit if you come into money or good people show up in your life. We tend to think of bad fruits as bad things external to ourselves that come to us: someone sues you,

you get robbed, or you have a car accident—things of that nature.

But we use this category of "fruits" here to also describe how you are feeling in your heart in an experience. The good fruits or bad fruits that occur *inside* of you, those interior experiences, St. Ignatius calls "consolations and desolations." His principles of consolations and desolations equally apply to the terms "good fruits" and "bad fruits." Consolations and desolations are feelings and perceptions that happen to you inside your heart, and can happen to you in the midst of your discernment and after you have discerned. Though fruits more accurately describe an external happening, we will use these terms interchangeably here, since the same principles generally apply.

Consolations describe the positive indicia of the Holy Spirit's presence in a situation. Consolations, or good fruits, are that which the Holy Spirit brings when you are doing God's will. They are "love, joy, peace, patience, kindness, goodness, faithfulness, gentleness, self-control" (Gal. 5:22-23). Peace is probably the most telling, the greatest good fruit or consolation, for Jesus said, "Peace I leave with you; my peace I give to you" (John 14:27). A consolation is "every increase in faith, hope and love, and all interior joy that invites and attracts to what is heavenly and to the salvation of one's soul . . ." (*Spiritual Exercises*, no. 316). A consolation can be a strong, overwhelming, positive emotion, like filling up with love. It can also be a sense of very quiet peacefulness.

If those are the consolations or spiritual good fruits, then what are the desolations, the spiritual bad fruits, which are signs that something is not from God or is not His will? Just the opposite of the consolations, really. Desolations include turmoil (lack of peace), anxiety, and restlessness. Desolations, Ignatius says, are "a darkness of soul, turmoil of spirit, inclination to what is low and earthly, restlessness arising from many disturbances which lead to lack of faith, lack of hope, lack of love. The soul is wholly slothful, tepid, sad, and separated, as it were, from its Creator and Lord" (*Spiritual Exercises*, Rule 4).

In simplest terms, a desolation is a lack of peace, which can range from frank and brutal torment to just an "off" feeling, the doldrums, a sense that something is not good or right.

So, the signs of the presence of a Holy Spirit, the spirit of God (a consolation, or good fruit) "fit with the teaching of the Church; [they are] serious, gives light to the soul, docility, discretion: no hurriedness or exaggerations; humble thoughts; confidence in God, rightness of intention, patience in suffering, self denial, sincerity and simplicity in conduct . . . great desire to imitate Christ in all things . . . gentleness, kindness," while the signs of the evil spirit, that which is not of God (a desolation, or bad fruit), are: "(the opposite of the above)—spirit of falseness or lie, suggestion of useless things, curious things, impertinent things, darkness, restlessness of the soul, a bold obstinate spirit, many indiscretions, pride, lack of hope, disobedience, vanity, self-satisfaction, impatience, rebellion of the passions, hypocrisy, pretense, attachment to earthly things, forgetfulness of Christ and of imitating [H]im, a false charity, including bitter zeal, indiscretion" (William G. Most, *Discernment of Spirits*).

The fruits of an experience are seldom only one thing or the other, black or white. That is why we need to discern, to sift them apart, because if it were all crystal clear and just one thing or the other, we would know what to do without any hesitation.

If you experience desolations, you can be assured that desolations are never directly from God. Desolations come from a dark spirit, namely, Satan. The devil is watching you and gives you desolations to discourage you and confuse you about God's will for your life.

Consolations, on the other hand, may be from God, or they may be from Satan. What? A feeling of peace might not be of God, you say? That can indeed be the case. How can that be?

St. Ignatius taught that this is because a mature Christian would likely be able to see the difference between a desolation (clearly from Satan) and a consolation (more presumptively from God). Because of that, Satan is more likely to have success working for the ruin of a devout soul by creating "false consolations" as opposed to outright desolations. Satan uses desolations more often on souls that are less devout, less faithful, less seeking, because he thinks that some bad feelings or some bad times will be enough to break that soul away from God's plan.

For someone who is more attuned to God's voice, or who is more steadfast in their faithfulness and perseverance, Satan's better tool is not desolations, which a devout soul would more easily see through as being from Satan. Satan has a better chance of influencing the devout soul with the confusion of a false consolation.

A false consolation can be a seemingly good thing that happens to you, but it is not really from God's hand. Worldly things, like money, fame, and notoriety, while they might be blessings from God, could also be from Satan. Even a peace could be Satan laying off you for a while, to try to influence you.

A false consolation that comes but that is not of God will at some point or in some way reveal that Satan is really behind it. Green calls that revealing the "tail of the snake," that is, unmasking the source as being from Satan and not God (Green, p. 128). The way to test whether something is a true or false consolation is to test fruits as St. Ignatius suggests: "If the beginning and middle and end . . . are wholly good and directed to what is entirely right, it is a sign that they are from" God (*Spiritual Exercises*, no. 333). The beginning refers to the circumstances from which the consolation occurs (what was happening when the consolation came to you). The middle is the experience of the consolation itself (what exactly was it, what happened). The end refers to where the consolation leads you (what fruits flowed from it).

You need to know that while God does not send them, God may allow or use the desolations or false consolations that Satan brings to us as a way for God to direct us and shape our growth. He does not send them, but He may allow them, and He will use them for your good, if you let Him.

When it comes to discerning fruits, what you really want is long-term good fruits or consolations, not fleeting good results or fleeting moments of feeling peaceful or better. You want to see over time that something indeed is a good fruit, bringing forth good, lasting effects in your life. You are not looking for short-term gains but long-term gains, to put it in economic terms. Generally, the mark of a true spiritual direction is that it is continuing over time. That reveals the will of God, when there are enduring true consolations, and good fruits, about the issue you are discerning.

Spiritual Direction/Advice. God speaks to us through other godly people, especially priests and religious. If you take questions about your life to a priest and ask for his wisdom and counsel, you should approach it as the Lord speaking to you through the person of the priest. God might speak to your heart about your situation in a priest's homily that many other people are hearing too, but which really answers specific concerns about which you are praying right now. God might speak to you through something Father says to you in the confessional that tells you which way to go on an issue. God might speak to you through counseling you get from a lay spiritual advisor. You need to be open to the wisdom of those holy advisors God has placed around you, wisdom which is given to them by God. If you are open to it, what they are saying could be God talking to you through them.

The Bible says that you should "seek, and you will find; knock, and it will be opened to you" (Matt. 7:8). This certainly applies to asking God to reveal His will in your life when you seek out spiritual direction.

Signs. Signs are occurrences, including supernatural occurrences, that appear in your life as a seeming answer to prayer, or perhaps surprising, unexpected occurrences which are imbued with meaning just for you. Things like visions (seeing something), locutions (hearing something audibly), inner locutions ("hearing" something in your own head but not in an audible voice), words of knowledge (factual or more-detailed insights), miraculous or unexplainable experiences, even coincidences can all fit into this category. Many of us will never experience such things, but they can and do happen. They can be from God, or may be from Satan or from our own imaginations.

Signs in particular must be very closely scrutinized, but they can definitely be a way in which God reveals His will to you. The Church has many resources on the discernment of signs and wonders. People who have unexplainable religious experiences are to submit their experience to the Church's scrutiny, so the Church has built up a treasury of knowledge on discerning if a vision or a locution is really of God or from another source (like a hallucination or the devil). St. Ignatius's *Spiritual Exercises* encompasses the discernment of signs as coming from the spirit of God or from the spirit of Satan. Not every "spirit" or influence on you is from God. If something is not from God, it can have only one of three sources: others, you, or Satan. Green calls it "the world, the flesh, and the devil" (Green, p. 153). The Church directs us to be very careful about the source of signs and wonders.

A sign could be something as profound and unusual as God actually speaking directly to you in an audible voice. He did it to Adam and to Moses, and to the disciples at the

Transfiguration, and He could do it to you, too. Or it could be something much more commonplace and subject to interpretation (like receiving a rose unexpectedly in response to praying a St. Thérèse novena). Signs have to be read and tested with skepticism because they can be your imagination, or the result of other people's actions or influence, or even the work of the devil. But they can be the revelation of the will of God also, so you have to be open to see and test such signs, preferably with a spiritual advisor, should they occur.

How can you know when a sign, a voice, or some event is from a dark source as opposed to God? Guillet suggests that a man will know when a dark influence is upon him because "the voice does not come from the man himself, but from a source that is disquieting—more rational and stronger than he, more tenacious, more aware of his plans, better informed than he regarding the tendencies of his own heart . . ." (Guillet, p. 18).

Never forget that the devil is capable of performing seemingly "holy" or good signs and wonders. He often masquerades in ways that seem good or even holy in order to lead us in the wrong direction. And then when the situation does not work out because it was really a falsehood from him, Satan hopes that the discouragement we feel will lead to "the abandonment of our whole commitment to the Lord. This, of course, is precisely what the evil spirit desires, and he is willing to sing Gregorian chant to accomplish it" (Green, p. 151).

Particularly with signs, you have to be very circumspect about the source of the sign. A spiritual director is the best resource for help if you experience any unusual occurrence or event that you think is a sign from God. Your spiritual advisor will likely use the tools the Church has gathered, like St. Ignatius's method for the discernment of spirits, to determine what the more likely source of your sign is: from God, from you, from others, or from Satan.

Conclusion. These are the ten fundamental ways in which you try to collect data or evidence so as to ascertain God's will. You gather data from all these sources and then discern if it is God talking to you in them. First you determine their source, if the source is indeed God. You then line up all your God-given data in these areas and see what God seems to be "saying" about your situation.

If, upon weighing all the data from these areas that seem to have God as their source, the answer to your question from God appears to be Him saying "no" to you on your issue or question, then you certainly don't do the thing you were contemplating, because it is likely not God's will for you. At the very least, you certainly don't do the thing now, and you should not consider doing it until you can collect more data, discern more, or discern better.

But if you line up your question or decision with all these things and everything seems to say "yes," then you may go ahead and act, if in an exercise of your free will you wish to do so. That's God's will for you; you can do what you will now, since it is in accord with His will.

When you do your discernment, you may see that some of these categories speak to you more than others. That makes sense. In deciding whether some of these sources of God's will are better for you in your discernment, keep in mind that God knows and treats each of us like a child, and "talks" to each of us, reveals his specific will for our lives, in a unique way, based on our personal traits and gifts. God will reveal His will to you as an individual. For example, for someone who is skeptical, intellectual, logical, and easily spooked by unexplainable things, God might not send such a person sparkly angels, talk to him in an audible voice, or give him visions. Rather, God might talk to such a person through Scripture, through the Liturgy of the Word, and through spiritual advisors. Such a person more accurately sees God's will from the categories of Scripture, church teaching, reason, fruits, and spiritual direction than in signs and wonders. This is because God really wants you to "hear" Him, so He will try to get through to you in the ways that reach you best, and those are not the same for everyone.

Discernment can sometimes seem like trying to read tea leaves, and that there is very little to go on. But if you keep your eyes, ears, and heart open, you often find that God is actually bombarding you all the time with clues to His will for you. If you are still confused, here is a tip: once you believe you have discerned God's will in a situation, act on it. After you have discerned on an issue, and you have made the decision, then you should act on it. Once you have made the decision, it is the aftereffects of the decision that will give you greater understanding if what you are doing is God's will. Once you act on the decision, you will either feel better or worse about it. You will experience consolations and/or desolations, good fruits and bad fruits. Remember, most actions yield both. If your action was God's will, generally more things will start to fall into place, you will have peace, and good fruits will come from it. So the best way to test God's will is to discern and then act. He will let you know by what occurs in response to your action whether you are on the right path now, in His view.

After there has been discernment, there should be what Green calls "certitude," that is, a certainty that is sufficient to allow one to act, to step out in faith, even courageously (Green, p. 67). While you might not understand God's will completely, your certainty is not of your reason or your mind. What you have certainty in is your faith, that God is leading you and will continue to reveal Himself to you if you keep an open heart. It's a trust in the Lord, not a trust in your own understanding.

You need to trust because here is the thing about discernment: you can never be 100 percent sure of what God's will is in any given situation. The only thing you can ever really know 100 percent is the dogmas of the Church. So if you are someone who is going to look for God's will in your life, you had better make some degree of uncertainty your friend. You must come to accept that complete clarity is seldom given by God, because the lack of it teaches us to trust in Him and in ourselves, and to move in faith. That is how we grow. And that is what God really wants, our trust in Him, and our growth as Christians. But even so, there will never be enough clarity about God's will for you to act properly unless you do all this work, and really seek all the information you need from all the above sources, in order to discern His will properly.

Another thing to keep in mind is that discernment is ongoing. God reveals His will in parts, like the unfolding of a story. He doesn't usually let you read the final chapter in advance. So in most decisions you do need to keep checking back to make sure you are still on the right track. As time goes by, more things occur, consolations and desolations come, good and bad fruits show up, new feelings develop, new insights are drawn, and those are all ways to see if you are on the right path or if God is trying to tell you that you took the wrong turn at the fork in the road as far as His will was concerned.

As Green says, "the final test of our discernment is in the living of the choice we . . . make" (Green, p. 194). What you do is discern, and then offer up your choice to God for His confirmation and approval. What will ensue is either consolation or desolation, and then you can either correct your course or continue on. Discernment is always ongoing, and therefore God will present you with opportunities for correcting your course, if you are always discerning and keeping an open heart, with your ear attuned to His voice. As time goes on and there remains consistent peace about the direction in which you are moving, then you have the best sign of God's will for you.

The bottom line is that if you are seeking God's will, He will be there for you as you travel the path. His will is always and most importantly that you love Him and want to be with Him. St. Augustine's motto was "Love God, and then do what you will," because if you love God and what He wills for you, then in doing what you will, you *are* doing His will, because you are in line with Him and doing what He wills (that you love Him).

Now that we are armed with how to look for manifestations of God's will in our lives in general, let's apply what we have learned to the most important decision you need to make in life, if you are called to the married state of life, and that is discerning God's will in the selection of your spouse.

Chapter 4

Discerning the Call to Marriage with a Specific Person

Discernment is a process that can be applied to any decision of your life. For a person of faith, it is of the utmost importance to use discernment when you are making those life-changing, critical decisions in life that will take you down one road or another. Deciding whom to marry is certainly one of those ultimate decisions in life that merit all the discernment you can give to it. Let's take these methods for discernment and see how we can gather data with which to discern God's will on whether or not you are called to marry a particular person.

Does God really have a specific will for your selection of a spouse? Perhaps before you answer that question, you might first consider whether every single moment and every single decision of your life has God's will superimposed on it. For example, does God have a specific will from all eternity that my next parking space is on the right or left side of the street? Probably not. But nothing is too small to take to Him in prayer, so if I pray, "Lord, I need a space on the right side of the street," and one appears, it was His will, and by His providence He gave it to me.

But there are some important life specifics that definitely have His specific will about them, and choice of a spouse is one of them. God wants input on your decision concerning your spouse because of the sacramental relationship the two of you will have with Him in marriage. But does God have one and only one person in mind for you to marry, just one soul mate, a person that God had chosen just for you from all eternity, that you and only you are meant to be joined with in the vocation of marriage? That's a question we might never be able to fully answer in this world.

There is a wonderful Jewish fable that goes something like this: Whenever a baby is born, the angels in heaven get together and try to figure out who in the world will be that baby's spouse. And the angels debate for and against their choices as to who they think would be the right spouse for this baby when the baby grows up. They fight and argue until God has heard enough of their debate, and He comes in to settle the matter. And God Himself selects who will be that person's spouse, and to show the angels the wisdom of whom He has selected, wills that the person will know or date or be in love with each of the angels' selections first, before God sends His selection to the person. Then all the angels will understand God's wisdom in why all of their choices of a spouse were not correct and His was the perfect match.

That story has a lot of appeal. God has far greater wisdom than we or the angels do. Who better than God to select your unique partner, the helpmate who is most suitable for you? We have seen already that there is support for the view there is one and only one person you are called to marry, based on the creation story in Genesis. But the "one and only" theory does not, however, take into account situations where someone has a happy Catholic marriage (presumably with a spouse selected by God), and then one spouse dies, and the surviving spouse goes on to remarry in another happy, Catholic marriage, also a sacrament sanctioned by God. In that case, it appears that God had more than one spouse in mind for that person (one at a time, of course).

So we can't know for sure if there is one and only one person for each of us, but we can be assured that if we are called to marriage, the person is out there somewhere. Out of all the men or women in the world, which one is going to be the one whom God has selected, sent, and approved to be with you and Him in the sacrament of marriage? That is what this discernment is all about.

When God brings such a person into your life, choosing that person is completely up to you. Might you discern it wrong, and miss the right person? Yes. Might God still use your mistake and might you exercise your free will and still marry someone else later and go on and have a happy life (i.e., with blessings by God)? Sure, for God works together all things (even our mistakes and misjudgments) for the good of us, who love Him. But just because some other person eventually comes along and you marry them does not mean that they were the person God willed for you, formed as the right helpmate for you. Of course, you will never really know all that until you get to heaven, and all is revealed about your life to you.

This chapter is focused on how you (you alone at this point) gather the data or raw material that you need to discern the will of God for your life as it concerns a particular person being your potential spouse. We are talking here about "solo" discernment: you, without the influence of your partner, asking, seeking, listening for what God's will is for you, for your life, concerning marriage. As we have seen, marriage is a service vocation, and you are not called to the vocation alone. You will be called with another person. In a sense, then, you get only 50 percent of the total discernment. We will talk more about that in Chapter 12 on "communal discernment," or discerning together with your partner what God is saying to the both of you. What this chapter is about is gathering the evidence about your 50 percent, your half, of the discernment. Presumably, your partner is doing similar discernment, and God is moving in his or her life as well. The goal of solo discernment is to be as clear as you can about what God is saying to you before you mix things up by talking to your partner about how God is leading him or her. You need to have as much certitude as possible on your half before you come together to see where God is leading you as a couple.

This question of discerning the call to marriage presupposes that there is something to discern. These actions and questions are for when you have someone in mind. This presupposes that you have met someone about whom there is something to discern. The issue needs to be joined first before you go through all of this. There needs to be a context in which to listen for God's will concerning marriage.

If you are reading this chapter, you already know that you are on a serious journey. You start out with meeting someone. You date. You date more seriously. You date exclusively. You begin to question what God has in store for your future. You discern alone. You discern together. You either break up or you get engaged. You participate in Pre-Cana and Engaged Encounter. And if everything still says "yes," you get married. That is the path you are on. Even if you are on the first step of that path, that is where this path can lead to, if that is what God wills for your life. So even if you are going on a first date with someone, this is in reality serious business because of where it can lead.

Once you have someone in mind, whether it's someone who is just going out with you on a first date or whether you have been dating for a while, it's time to arm yourself with the list of discernment "tools" set out in Chapter 3. It's time to see how God's will can be manifested in the most important discernment there is in life, if you are called to the married state: the discernment of your spouse.

So let's use those ten areas we learned about and see how you can examine them to discern if someone is your God-given spouse.

Holy Scripture. What does God's Word reveal about whom you are to marry, within God's will? What does Scripture tell us about marriage, and whom to marry, for that matter? There are many references to marriage in the Bible that we can look at to get some guidelines for who it is you are to marry. Let's take a look at them.

The first answer to the question of whom you are looking for is provided in 2 Corinthians 6:14: "Do not be mismated with unbelievers." Another translation is: "Do not be yoked with those who are different, with unbelievers." If you are a believer, you are not to yoke yourself, join yourself, with someone who is not a believer. If the person you are discerning is not a Christian, if they do not believe that Christ is the Son of God and the Savior of the world, and their Savior specifically, then you have to question very seriously whether they can be God's chosen spouse for you. It might be that in knowing you, they may come to believe in Christ, and that would be a wonderful result of your relationship. While the Church does not necessarily prohibit a marriage between a Catholic and a non-Christian but might permit it in some circumstances, you would have to explore very seriously whether marriage to a non-Christian is God's will for you, since it would seem to be contrary to God's Word, and His will will agree first and foremost with His Word.

Next, let's see what the Lord is saying to us in Matthew 19:3-12:

> And Pharisees came up to him and tested him by asking, "Is it lawful to divorce one's wife for any cause?" He answered, "Have you not read that he who made them from the beginning made them male and female, and said, 'For this reason a man shall leave his father and mother and be joined to his wife, and the two shall

become one'? So they are no longer two but one. What therefore God has joined together, let not man put asunder." They said to him, "Why then did Moses command one to give a certificate of divorce, and to put her away?" He said to them, "For your hardness of heart Moses allowed you to divorce your wives, but from the beginning it was not so. And I say to you: whoever divorces his wife, except for unchastity, and marries another, commits adultery; and he who marries a divorced woman, commits adultery."

The disciples said to him, "If such is the case of a man with his wife, it is not expedient to marry." But he said to them, "Not all men can receive this saying, but only those to whom it is given. For there are eunuchs who have been so from birth, and there are eunuchs who have been made eunuchs by men, and there are eunuchs who have made themselves eunuchs for the sake of the kingdom of heaven. He who is able to receive this, let him receive it."

Mark's Gospel gives the same material a slightly different treatment, in Mark 10:2-12:

And Pharisees came up and in order to test him asked, "Is it lawful for a man to divorce his wife?" He answered them, "What did Moses command you?" They said, "Moses allowed a man to write a certificate of divorce, and to put her away." But Jesus said to them, "For your hardness of heart he wrote you this commandment. But from the beginning of creation, 'God

made them male and female.' 'For this reason
a man shall leave his father and mother and be
joined to his wife, and the two shall become
one.' So they are no longer two but one. What
therefore God has joined together, let not man
put asunder."

And in the house the disciples asked him
again about this matter. And he said to them,
"Whoever divorces his wife and marries another, commits adultery against her; and if she
divorces her husband and marries another, she
commits adultery."

The Lord makes very clear how He sees divorce. These
verses really show that this marriage business is gravely serious, and that we really need to get it right the first time so
it will be the only time. If the person you are discerning is
not someone you think you can make it with for the whole
race, the long run, until you are parted by death, then he or
she is not the person that God has planned for you. You
really need to make sure someone shares this same view of
marriage.

Going back to the Gospel of Matthew, let's see what wisdom there is in Matthew 5:27-28:

"You have heard that it was said, 'You shall not
commit adultery.' But I say to you that every
one who looks at a woman lustfully has already
committed adultery with her in his heart."

Here, Jesus is reminding us of the sixth commandment,
and giving a real-life example of what is a violation of the
ninth commandment. Clearly, you are not to marry anyone
with whom your relationship would be adulterous. That
means anyone who in the eyes of God is already married. If

you think that you heaven-sent spouse is someone who is married, or is only separated at this point, or is civilly divorced but without a church annulment, you are mistaken.

But what about that second part, lusting in your heart for someone? While we will learn more about the discernment of sexual attraction in Chapter 9, if there is someone for whom your primary interest is sexual, then they are likely not God's chosen spouse for you. Again, God is not going to send you someone whom your thinking and fantasizing about would be a violation of the ninth commandment. If that is basically all that is drawing you to him or her, you had better move on, as attractive as they might appear to you. God would not send someone whom knowing would be for you to violate the ninth commandment.

There is further enlightenment in Luke 20:27-36:

> There came to him some Sadducees, those who say that there is no resurrection, and they asked him a question, saying, "Teacher, Moses wrote for us that if a man's brother dies, having a wife but no children, the man must take the wife and raise up children for his brother. Now there were seven brothers; the first took a wife, and died without children; and the second and the third took her, and likewise all seven left no children and died. Afterward the woman also died. In the resurrection, therefore, whose wife will the woman be? For the seven had her as wife."
>
> And Jesus said to them, "The sons of this age marry and are given in marriage; but those who are accounted worthy to attain to that age and to the resurrection from the dead neither marry nor are given in marriage, for they cannot die any more, because they are equal to angels and are sons of God, being sons of the resurrection.

This text reminds us that marriage is an earthly matter. It might seem really important and all-encompassing when you are seeking it in your life as your vocation, as your life's work, but marriage is really only an earthly treasure that is passing away, like everything in this world. It is something that is of this world, not of the next. Serving a spouse in the vocation of marriage might well be your way of salvation, your "ticket" as it were, to getting to heaven, but there is no marriage in heaven, Jesus taught us.

The message here may be: if there is a person you are discerning that you are so wrapped up in, and in the earthly aspects of your relationship (how they look, being together, having fun together, the good times, your earthly future together, the babies you would have, your sexual attraction), you might want to be circumspect over whether they are indeed the person God has sent. Sometimes someone comes along that is a distraction to you from seeing, from keeping your eyes on the real prize, that is, a life in heaven someday with God. A perfectly nice person, even a good person, can still be such a distraction for you.

Ask yourself: has being with this person taken me away from spiritual practices and devotions? Am I praying less because our dating leaves me no time? Am I finding myself confronted with near occasions of sexual sins because I am dating this person? Those types of things would suggest that you might be in a relationship that is about the earthly experience, and not one that will lead you to and support you in what we can call "the higher purposes," that is, knowledge of God and getting to heaven. God is going to send you someone who will help you stay focused on the higher purposes, you can be assured of that.

Moving on to the Gospel of John, we see what the Lord has to say in Chapter 8:1-11:

> Jesus went to the Mount of Olives. Early in the
> morning he came again to the temple; all the

people came to him, and he sat down and taught them. The scribes and the Pharisees brought a woman who had been caught in adultery, and placing her in the midst they said to him, "Teacher, this woman has been caught in the act of adultery. Now in the law Moses commanded us to stone such. What do you say about her?" This they said to test him, that they might have some charge to bring against him. Jesus bent down and wrote with his finger on the ground. And as they continued to ask him, he stood up and said to them, "Let him who is without sin among you be the first to throw a stone at her." And once more he bent down and wrote with his finger on the ground. But when they heard it, they went away, one by one, beginning with the eldest, and Jesus was left alone with the woman standing before him. Jesus looked up and said to her, "Woman, where are they? Has no one condemned you?" She said, "No one, Lord." And Jesus said, "Neither do I condemn you; go, and do not sin again."

What does this have to say about whom you should marry? This Scripture reminds us that we are all sinners, and every person that we discern also is a sinner. As you get to know someone, you might learn things about them, their past, their sexual history, other areas of their life, that might not be all you might hope. When you are a devout Catholic, there is a perfectionism that can sometimes set in, so that the person you are looking for has to be perfect, can have no flaws whatsoever. What this Scripture says to us is that everyone has sinned, and everyone can be forgiven by God's mercy if they seek it. And you need to have a merciful and forgiving heart as well, because you are a sinner too.

If you are discerning someone and you find out there is a past area of sin in their life, particularly in the area of sexual sin, don't be too quick to reject them. The Lord can make new the heart of someone who has come back to Him seeking His forgiveness. While there might be things that you feel you can't ever deal with, don't decide such a thing too quickly. Perhaps the person you are falling for has the sin of abortion in her past. Perhaps he fathered a child out of wedlock. Perhaps they have a sexual history that left them with a venereal disease. Does that mean they are not God's chosen spouse for you? Maybe, or maybe not. God is reminding us here that all have sinned, some in one way, some in another, but that He can renew us, redeem us, and make us whole again. You need only think of Mary Magdalene to see that God can redeem anyone and make them worthy of the highest calling of following Him. Maybe it is in this person's broken and sinful past that there is a real lesson for you about God's mercy and His forgiveness that you need to learn as part of your path to salvation. The moral is: don't expect perfection out of your spouse that you don't have yourself, and which even God has not required. Look at what is in the person's heart now, and go from here. Confide in a good priest that you trust who is experienced in these matters, listen to his opinion, and pray about it.

There are two more verses of the New Testament that are particularly illuminating in the call to whom you might marry. First, let's take a look at Paul's first letter to the Corinthians, Chapter 7:1-5:

> Now concerning the matters about which you wrote. It is well for a man not to touch a woman. But because of the temptation to immorality, each man should have his own wife and each woman her own husband. The husband should give to his wife her conjugal rights, and likewise the wife to her husband. For the

wife does not rule over her own body, but the husband does; likewise the husband does not rule over his own body, but the wife does. Do not refuse one another except perhaps by agreement for a season, that you may devote yourselves to prayer; but then come together again, lest Satan tempt you through lack of self-control.

If you are discerning your future spouse, you have to ask: is this someone I am willing to submit to, to put myself under their authority? Your body will belong in a real sense to your spouse; you will be one flesh with your spouse. Is this a person you can be that with? If you can't say that, they are not the person that God is sending for you.

Perhaps the greatest verse of Scripture about whom you are called to marry may be that found in Ephesians, Chapter 5. This verse gives the great commands of what Christian marriage requires of the spouses. By looking at what the Lord will require of you in marriage, you should get good insight as to whether someone might be His chosen spouse for you:

Be subject to one another out of reverence for Christ. Wives, be subject to your husbands, as to the Lord. For the husband is the head of the wife as Christ is the head of the church, his body, and is himself its Savior. As the church is subject to Christ, so let wives also be subject in everything to their husbands. Husbands, love your wives, as Christ loved the church and gave himself up for her, that he might sanctify her, having cleansed her by the washing of water with the word, that he might present the church to himself in splendor, without spot or wrinkle or any such thing, that she might be holy and without blemish. Even so husbands should love their wives as their own bodies. He who loves his wife loves himself. For no man ever hates his own flesh, but nourishes and cherishes it, as Christ does the church, because we are members of his body. "For this reason a man shall leave his father and mother and be joined to his wife, and the two shall become one flesh." This mystery is a profound one, and I am saying that it refers to Christ and the church; however, let each one of you love his wife as himself, and let the wife see that she respects her husband. (Eph. 5:21-33)

"Be subject to one another." Ask yourself: is this a person that I can lay my own will down for, for their good, even over my own? Whether you are a man or woman, you need to ask that about the person you are dating.

This verse challenges women to ask: is this a man I respect? Is this a man I believe is truly following Christ himself, such that he himself is "subject to Christ"? If that is the case, then ask, can I subject myself to this man's leadership, particularly in matters of faith? The man is the spiritual head of the household—"the husband is the head of the wife." This is not some anti-feminist statement. God's Word is saying that, in the family, ultimately there has to be someone in charge, and that is the husband. The marriage and the family must have spiritual leadership, and that is to come from the husband. God's command to you as a wife is to subject yourself to your husband. If that is the case, then the question is this: is this a man to whom I can entrust my spirit, before whom I can lay down my own formidable will, and let him lead me and our family, because I am assured that Christ is leading him?

If you are discerning whether a man is possibly God's chosen spouse for you, you have to be able to say "yes," that you not only respect this man, and believe that he is following Christ, but that you can also follow him, let him lead, when he is acting in his God-given role as spiritual head of your household, and when he is following Christ. If you can't do that with this man, he is not God's man for you.

A wife can let her husband lead—will willingly lay down her will to him, subject herself to him—because she knows he is following Christ. She lets him lead her because Christ is leading him, and Christ therefore is leading them both. All of those links must be there and if they are not, then this man is not your husband.

The Lord wants for you to have a marriage that reflects Ephesians, Chapter 5. These are his commands to you as a wife. If you cannot live those commands with the man you are discerning, then he is not God's spouse for you.

As for the men, if you are looking to discern a woman, ask yourself this: do I love her as Christ loves the Church? Am I willing to sacrifice myself, my life, for her? This is the Lord's command to husbands, and it is a command—to love that much, with that much self-sacrifice, with a total out-pouring of yourself. Because that is what God commands if you are to marry, if you don't love this woman with that level of self-sacrifice, then she is not your wife; she is not the woman God has chosen for you.

God will not send someone as your spouse with whom it is not possible for you to fulfill the commands of Ephesians, Chapter 5. If you can't pledge with assurance that you can follow the commands He gave you in this verse of Scripture, this person is not your spouse. While this holy Scripture is one you might want to argue with, it's a command. If you don't love in this way—if you cannot respond in this wholehearted fashion—the person is not the one sent by God for you to have in marriage.

Of course, you have to test these questions over time. You might not know on the first date whether you would lay down your life for a particular woman. But after dating six months or a year, you should have a good idea if you are even in the ballpark concerning your response to these commands. While this kind of respect for a man, or love for a woman, is something that grows over time, and even grows during marriage, and is in fact the ongoing challenge of marriage, eventually this is the test you are going to have to hold your partner, and yourself, up to. So you had best keep this test in your mind at all times in the dating process.

For a man seeking a wife, a great insight in the Bible on what you are looking for is found in the last book of Proverbs, which outlines what a good wife is. It provides almost a checklist for what a man should be looking for in a wife:

A good wife who can find?
        She is far more precious than jewels.
The heart of her husband trusts in her,
        and he will have no lack of gain.
She does him good, and not harm,
        all the days of her life.
She seeks wool and flax,
        and works with willing hands.
She is like the ships of the merchant,
        she brings her food from afar.
She rises while it is yet night
        and provides food for her household and
tasks for her maidens.
She considers a field and buys it;
        with the fruit of her hands she plants a vineyard.
She girds her loins with strength
        and makes her arms strong.
She perceives that her merchandise is profitable.
        Her lamp does not go out at night.
She puts her hands to the distaff,
        and her hands hold the spindle.
She opens her hand to the poor,
        and reaches out her hands to the needy.

She is not afraid of snow for her household,
>for all her household are clothed in scarlet.
She makes herself coverings;
>her clothing is fine linen and purple.
Her husband is known in the gates,
>when he sits among the elders of the land.
She makes linen garments and sells them;
>she delivers girdles to the merchant.
Strength and dignity are her clothing,
>and she laughs at the time to come.
She opens her mouth with wisdom,
>and the teaching of kindness is on her tongue.
She looks well to the ways of her household,
>and does not eat the bread of idleness.
Her children rise up and call her blessed;
>her husband also, and he praises her:
"Many women have done excellently,
>but you surpass them all."
Charm is deceitful, and beauty is vain,
>but a woman who fears the LORD is to be
>praised.
Give her of the fruit of her hands,
>and let her works praise her in the gates.
>(Prov. 31:10–31)

A woman who will be a good wife, according to God's Word, is one who is diligent, hard-working, industrious, capable of many different tasks and has many skills, is trustworthy, charitable and kind, resourceful, thrifty, good to all, efficient, cheerful, wise, and reflects well on you and honors your household. Is the woman you are discerning like that? If so, she might well be the one God has sent.

The verse also warns that things that the world might value, like physical beauty and worldly charms, are fleeting, but it is a woman who "fears the Lord" that you should be looking for.

God has provided you with a clear blueprint against which you can compare any woman whom you are discerning. If the woman you are discerning does not pray, does not have a proper fear of the Lord, does not reflect the all-around traits the wife of Proverbs does, but rather seems to be more about the things of this world, like her looks, dress, hair, make-up, socializing, parties, amusements and gossip, you have to ask yourself whether God would really send someone to you to be your spouse if she is not matching up with God's own description of what is a good wife for a man, including a man like you.

"He that hath found a good wife, hath found a good thing, and shall receive pleasure from the LORD. He that driveth away a good wife, driveth away a good thing" (Prov. 18:22, Douay-Rheims Bible). So make sure you recognize a woman who would be a good wife when you see her, and take great care to not reject such a woman if God sends one into your life. You might be turning away God's most precious gift to you.

Men seem to like checklists and action. Women are more attuned to feelings and emotions. God's Word has something for the women, too. There is a beautiful verse of Scripture, from the book of Ruth, that describes the depth of emotion and commitment you should feel about any man you are contemplating as your husband. While Ruth speaks these words to her mother-in-law in the Bible, they show her commitment to be joined to her husband and his family. These are the words you should be able to say to the man with whom you are thinking of sharing the vocation of marriage:

> Ruth said, "Entreat me not to leave you or to return from following you; for where you go I will go, and where you lodge I will lodge; your people shall be my people, and your God my God; where you die I will die, and there will I

be buried. May the LORD do so to me and more also if even death parts me from you." (Ruth 1:16-17)

This is the depth of feeling and commitment that the sacrament of marriage requires of you. Is this a man you would leave your family and friends for? Is this a man you would change everything for, sacrifice everything for? Is this a man that you would follow to the ends of the earth, if that is where he needs to go? Is this a man who you want to be with at death?

Is this the man to whom you can say these things with all your heart? If so, it would appear you have found your treasure. If not, you need to look on until you can give yourself and your life this fully to the man whom God does have in mind for you.

There are also good clues in the Song of Songs, the only book of the Bible devoted to the exhortation of romantic love. The Song of Songs is a metaphor for God's love for us, Christ's love for the Church, but told in an analogy to human romantic love, so that we could have a framework in which to try to understand it. Who can understand how much God loves us? Human romantic love is the closest thing we have to the rapturous love that God has for each one of us. So read that book to get an idea of how you should feel about the person if they are the kind of spouse with whom God would want you to join yourself.

As we have now seen, there is much wisdom in God's Word on the selection of a spouse. God has not abandoned you and left you to find your own way in the darkness. These verses are some of the references in God's Word that inform on God's will for the selection of a holy spouse. You should read the Bible to look for God to speak to your heart further about finding your husband or wife.

Use the techniques from Chapter 3 for studying the Bible,

such as really listening to the readings at Mass, asking God to give you a word of Scripture that will address your concerns and answer your own questions about the person you are discerning. His Word will always guide you and never let you down.

Church Teaching. Now that we have seen what the Bible has to say about whom to marry, we turn to how the Catholic Church has applied that revelation. The Church, through the Catechism and its tradition, has a lot to say about whom you are to marry.

First, and foremost, the Church teaches that you can marry only someone who is free to be validly married in the Church as a sacrament. If they are not free, they probably are not sent from God to be your spouse, unless and until they can enter into a sacramental marriage. God would not send a spouse that is not free to marry in the Church. If the person you are discerning is not free to marry in the Church, then they are not your spouse, either not ever or, at the very least, not now.

To be your spouse, you have to have someone who can enter into a valid marriage as the Church considers validity. One thing that means is that they are open to any children that the Lord chooses to bless your marriage with. If someone holds a belief in the use of contraception, or is not open to children in your marriage (they say they don't want any kids, or are undecided about whether they do), then they are probably not the spouse that God intends for you, if you seek a sacramental marriage.

If they, in words or action, profess that they don't want children at all, that it is their intention to remain childless, the person is not your spouse. Openness to the blessing of children is a requirement of a valid sacramental marriage. A ground to ask for a Church annulment is that a spouse was not open to the blessing of children. The Church can conclude that such an attitude renders a marriage invalid. God would not send you someone who would not enter into a valid sacramental marriage with you as far as children are concerned.

The Church teaches that to be your spouse, the person does not necessarily have to be a baptized and confirmed Catholic, but they do have to be willing to live by all the moral teachings of the Church, and you have to confirm that they will not interfere with your (not their) promise to raise any children of your marriage in the Catholic faith.

While the Church allows marriage to a non-Catholic, it does not encourage it. And what does the Bible verse on being "equally yoked" suggest about marrying a non-Catholic? You need to search your heart and find out if, to you, that means someone has to be Catholic for you to marry them. If someone is Christian, but not Catholic, is that an "equal" enough yoke for you? For many devout Catholics, it will not be.

Are you secure enough in your faith that you can live day in, day out, with someone who does not hold all your beliefs, faith, and practices? Will being around someone who does not believe as you do drag you down? Are you able to be your own encouragement in the practice of the faith, since your spouse will not be able to be that for you? Will your faith be able to handle all the assaults that the world will bring on as well as any issues or debates your spouse might bring on? Will you be able to defend your faith should your spouse question or disagree with your beliefs and practices? Do you want to open yourself up to a life that will include these additional struggles in addition to all the other struggles that come with marriage?

You have to think about the future when it comes to marriage, and a Catholic marriage means an openness to children and a commitment to raising them in the faith. If you are the Catholic in the family and you marry a non-Catholic, you are signing up for a lifetime of answering questions like, "Why do I have to go to Mass? Dad doesn't have to go . . . Why do I have to go to confession? Dad doesn't go . . . Why should I believe that the Eucharist is Jesus? Dad doesn't believe that," and so on. Being raised in a household where Catholicism and some other faith are both present is confusing to children, that is certain. You have to think about the other lives that will be entrusted to you when selecting your spouse, and children are certainly one area where that is well demonstrated.

For a devout Catholic woman in particular, marrying a non-Catholic can be problematic, given the Lord's command to be subordinate to her husband. If you are mature in your faith, a devout practicing Catholic, and your man is Christian but not Catholic, in good conscience are you going to be able to submit to him on matters of faith, given that he will not be as versed in the teachings or foundations of that faith, since it is not his tradition? While someone who is Christian but not Catholic could be your spouse, you have to figure out for yourself if you consider that an equal yoke, and can obey the Lord's command in that situation.

There is always the question of conversion—that your man will convert to the Catholic faith in order for the two of you to marry in the Church. While that would be a good thing, and you might be an influence to bring him into the fullness of salvation through the sacraments of the Church, you still need to discern if you will be able to submit yourself to him even then.

It is rather like someone who has a postgraduate degree (you, as a mature Catholic) submitting herself in matters of faith to the guidance of someone with the equivalent of a grade-school education (a new convert to the faith). Every situation is different, and there might be a man who is so extraordinary in faith that he could convert, and his faith be such that you as the more mature Catholic could still submit to him. But that is not going to be the usual case.

As a Catholic woman, you do not want to be in the position of dragging your husband into the practices and beliefs of the Church. He is to lead, remember? Though this is often what happens, it is not the best solution to get engaged and then have the non-Catholic convert. Rather, if he wants to join the Church, then let the Holy Spirit lead him in his conversion, not because it is a way to be married to you. You want to avoid what might be called a "diamond ring" conversion—one party converting to Catholicism just to please the other, or their family. If his conversion is not just in form but a true call on his heart, let that happen without regard to you. It may be God's will that he become a Catholic. Thereafter discern if you are called to be married together.

As for the men, marrying a non-Catholic woman, or her converting as a condition of the marriage, might be somewhat less problematic. Who ever said life was fair? This is, again, because the husband is to be the spiritual head of the household. A Catholic husband can lead a non-Catholic wife, or a converting wife, in a way that is in accordance with God's command of Ephesians 5. A wife's command is to be subordinate, so for her to be in the position as the more mature Catholic, as the person with the presumably more-advanced faith, to join herself to a non-Catholic or a new convert husband, is more complicated.

There are countless examples of Catholic women who have led (or possibly dragged) their nonbelieving husbands to their salvation, and into heaven. But if you are not yet married, you should not seek to have this be your life experience. Scripture suggests that if you are already married to an unbeliever, you can remain as such, but you might do better not to seek out such a situation (see 1 Cor. 7:12-13; 2 Cor. 6:14). If God wants to convert a man or woman you care about, then by all means, help them, guide them, aid them, but let that be about their own faith experience, and not a ticket to getting a chance to marry you.

Similarly, there is the question of whether the person you are discerning is Catholic but not as devout as you are in the practice of the Catholic faith. If you are a devout Catholic woman—say, you attend daily Mass, say the rosary daily, go to confession every week, and are very active in your parish—and the man you are discerning is more of a "pew sitter"—fulfills his Sunday obligation for Mass but that's really it; he doesn't really have a prayer life, doesn't go to confession very often, and has no interest in any liturgical or charitable ministry—you have to ask yourself, is that someone you can be "equally yoked" with? Of course, this situation is one that is most worth working with, because there will never be a complete match in how faithful two people are, how their different faith paths have led and prepared them. We are all here to help each other on the path to salvation. But you have to ask yourself if someone will help and aid you, or potentially drag you backwards in your faith. Will that man who is a "Sundays-only" Catholic interfere with your attendance of daily Mass, which is the level at which your faith is functioning? Will he slowly chip away at that call you have to attend daily Mass, to accommodate his lifestyle? What would God think of that?

Whether someone who is not as devout as you are can still be your spouse is for you to discern, but it is a question that you have to look at very seriously. You want someone who not only really shares the faith with you, but who will make you more, make you better, in the practice of your faith. If someone is more lukewarm than you are, you have to ask how that is likely to occur.

The Lord does move in extraordinary ways, and it could be that over time, your non-Catholic, or converted, or "pew-sitting" partner will become a bulldog for the Catholic Church and its teachings, and even be an example for you in the faith. That could happen, and we all know of examples where it has occurred. So you will have to consider that very carefully if you find yourself in such a situation.

One thing the Church teaches that is completely clear is that the use of any form of artificial contraception is gravely immoral and a mortal sin (Catechism, para. 2370). You must find out whether your partner completely agrees with the Church's teaching and will live out that teaching fully in marriage. If the other person does not embrace the Church's teaching, you can and should instruct them in this matter of faith or see that they get that from a priest or the Catechism. Perhaps the reason God has brought you into his life is to help him with this struggle to understand and live by the teaching of the Church, and it is the good and Christian thing to do to help him on this issue. But you shouldn't marry him under such circumstances.

To have a sacramental marriage, both parties must be open to the unitive and procreative aspects of the sacrament. That means that both are open to all life that God will bless the union with, the fruit of marriage, which is children. The Church teaches that artificial contraception is a grave evil and a mortal sin. If the person you are thinking about marrying espouses the use of artificial birth control, in any form, then you must question if that person is God's will for you at this point. You might be able to instruct them on what the Church teaches, and if they are willing to prayerfully consider and submit to what the Church teaches, then you might discern further in the future, after you can be sure they have had a real change of heart and now accept and embrace the beauty of the Church's teaching.

If, after full instruction on the Church's teaching on contraception, someone still holds a contraceptive mentality—if they are going to insist upon the use of artificial contraception in any form in the marriage—then they are not your intended spouse. Artificial contraception in any form is a mortal sin, that is what the Church teaches; that is what you must know if they really believe and accept. In marriage, sex and all that surrounds it has to be one place where you and your spouse are in total agreement and completely on the same page. If there is any disagreement between you, how can you ever hope to become the one flesh that God commands you to be?

Can you even imagine the pain you would experience if your spouse wanted to introduce a mortal sin (contraception) into what is supposed to be the most intimate, sacred moment of your marriage? Can you imagine your spouse asking you to sin, and you agreeing to sin, in the midst of that sacredness? That is not God's will for you, and in your heart you know that.

Similarly, someone could harbor an anti-conceptive mentality in matters beyond the use of contraception itself. There are sexual practices that the world considers totally acceptable, even desirable, that are immoral because they are anti-conceptive acts. This would include oral sex to orgasm without vaginal intercourse, masturbation performed alone or together, or other sexual stimulation to orgasm without vaginal intercourse. All of these, while widely practiced "in the world," are in truth anti-conceptive practices, and thus are sinful, even in marriage. Why? Because each of these acts eliminates the possibility of conception, and every sexual act in a sacramental marriage must be open to the transmission of life, the possibility of conception (Catechism, para. 2370). As these actions do not, they are contraceptive acts, in essence, just like using birth control pills or condoms.

Anyone who wants anti-conceptive acts to be part of your marriage, or wants to engage in them premaritally, is not your heaven-sent spouse. Again, you can instruct such a person in the faith's teaching. You can encourage them to talk to a priest to understand why. You can encourage them to study Church teaching to better understand the beautiful gift of sexuality God has placed in us and understand the sacramental expression of it in marriage. But if someone does not accept and want to live in accordance with this most important Church teaching about marriage—that in sex you must be open to life in all your actions—then they are not your spouse. It is that simple.

No one said it was going to be easy discerning your Catholic spouse.

Similarly, if someone wants you to compromise your chastity premaritally, or is willing to compromise their own, even for you, he or she is not your spouse sent from God. While you must discern your sexual attraction to each other, the person that God has sent to you will be someone who honors your chastity, and if you are a virgin, honors your virginity, and would never ask you or consistently encourage you to sin in that area, if they are God's spouse for you. You must avoid any unbalanced relationship where one is willfully trying to convince the other to do something they should not.

All have fallen short of the glory of God, and we are all sinners, and by a certain age, probably most adults have committed some kind of sexual sin, either masturbation, premarital unchastity (petting, oral sex), or intercourse outside of marriage. Of course, the Lord can forgive it all, if you confess it in the sacrament of reconciliation. But that forgiveness requires that you amend your ways and keep yourself away from such sins now and in the future.

Especially with the person with whom God intends for you to live the fullness of the precious gift of your sexuality—your spouse—your "sex life" will be holy and chaste. Premarital chastity is a good indicator of whether a person will be able to live out marital chastity, but we will deal with that more in Chapter 9, on the discernment of sexual attraction.

As a member of the Catholic Church, you may feel that the Church tells you more about whom you cannot marry than about whom you can. But if you want to be joined in the sacrament of marriage, you can marry only someone free to marry in the Church. That means someone who has never been married before, someone who is widowed, or someone who has received a Church annulment if one is needed. If the person you are thinking of is not in one of those categories, the person is not in God's will for you to marry at this time. You should not expose yourself to the heartache of dating someone who is not free to marry in the faith. That is not God's will for you.

Ultimately, the Church is trying to point you to the person with whom you can most fully live the sacrament. Read paragraph 2365 of the Catechism. These are the words of St. John Chrysostom, and if you are a man, they are what you are looking to be able to say to a woman. If you can't say this to the woman that you are considering to share with in the marital vocation, then she is not your vocation:

> I have taken you in my arms, and I love you, and I prefer you to my life itself. For the present life is nothing, and my most ardent dream is to spend it with you in such a way that we may be assured of not being separated in the life reserved for us . . . . I place your love above all things, and nothing would be more bitter or painful to me than to be of a different mind than you.

Men, you should look for the woman to whom you can say these things. Women, you are looking for the man who is saying these things, in his words and in his actions, to you. If that is not what you are finding, you had best move on.

The Church, through its teachings, has much guidance and wisdom as to whom you should marry. Turn to the Catechism and you will find a lot of information about who might be your spouse.

Conscience. Your own conscience can reveal important information to you on what is God's will in the selection of your spouse. There might be matters that are not explicitly covered by a section of the Catechism, or by a verse of the Bible. But your own conscience can inform you that a person may or may not be God's chosen spouse for you.

Your conscience is what you are always listening to, like a radio tuned into God's wavelength that is always playing in the background. And it's an excellent tool when it comes to discerning your spouse as you date and spend time together.

Here's an example of how conscience can help you, drawn from my own life. I dated a man who was in his forties, was a faithful every-Sunday Catholic, was very good-hearted to everyone, very charitable, and engaged in many acts of mercy for those around him. He was not really as devout as I was in his practice of the faith, but it was clear to me that his focus was on the Lord and he was trying to do the right thing. He seemed in many ways to be the sort of man God might be wanting me to discern more closely as a potential husband.

But when we got to the point where he explained his sexual history to me, I learned that he had had intercourse with a shocking number of women. I learned that with the Catholic woman he dated just a few months before me, they had not been able to maintain chastity, and his idea of chastity before marriage even now was that as long as you didn't engage in intercourse, you were "okay."

He had confessed all this to God and been forgiven, and there was nothing in the Bible or in Church teaching that would tell me that a man with such a past could not be a husband to me. But my own conscience told me something else. It told me this was a man who had not honored his body as a temple of the Holy Spirit, and who still did not see his body that way. It told me that he did not see women in general as being temples of the Holy Spirit. He quite recently had not been able to maintain chastity, and was misinformed on what premarital chastity actually requires. Given my particular background, I discerned with my own conscience, with my own inherent sense of right and wrong, that this was not the man that God had sent for me, as God wants me to be equally yoked, and I did not see this as a man who would honor my chastity or appreciate and understand the gift of sexuality in any marriage between us.

And I was duty bound to follow my conscience, so I stopped seeing him.

Nothing the Bible states, or the Church teaches, told me there was anything wrong with marrying a man with this history, but my conscience told me otherwise—that for me, that was not what God wanted for *my* life. The purity of the sexuality between me and my husband, the full expression of it, the gift that our sexuality is each for the other, is pivotal to me in marriage. So my sense of right and wrong told me that my husband has a sexual history that honors him and me. This man did not have that, and so I discerned he was not my husband. And I am glad I did that, because it would have been a grave mismatch, and I would have defeated God's real call for my life concerning marriage.

So when someone comes into your life, you need to have your radar tuned in to your own conscience, through which God may be trying to guide you concerning the person who is to be your spouse.

Reason. Your sense of reason, using the brain that God gave you, is a powerful tool in discerning your spouse. While the heart knows what reason cannot, God gave us both a brain and a heart, and we are supposed to use them both in hearing His will for us in this important area. Too often in love, people are so swept up in what they think their heart is saying—those intense feelings of being in love, or sexual attraction. But God gave you a brain, and you need to use it. In fact, the heart is to be subordinate to the mind when it comes to making important life decisions.

This is the realm where the wisdom and reason of human psychology come up. What kind of person do you need? Do you need someone who is neat? Do you need someone who is organized? Do you need someone who will not nag you? Such "are we compatible" questions are one of the ways you can use your reason to discern.

Also, reason can be used to analyze whether logically this could be the person for you. What if a woman is really everything you have ever wanted? Say your "list" for the perfect wife is a devout Catholic, who embraces and lives fully the teachings of the Church, has never been married, even is the answer to your prayers to marry a virgin, has your same chastity convictions, is pretty, in nice shape, wants children, has a good job and a wonderful family of origin, is funny, a good housekeeper, loves to cook, and is adored by everyone. Your gift of reason, your own sense of the situation, ought to tell you that this could well be the woman God has sent for you. Similarly, if reason tells you someone is not some of the things you have long held as extremely important to you, then they may well not be the one for you.

Your reason will tell you things that your heart does not. For example, a man who works 75 hours a week, in a distant city, and who has serious business concerns, a bit of a drinking problem, and whose mother dislikes you already, might not be the man you are supposed to marry.

God gave you a brain. Don't be so fogged by your emotions that you forget to use this very important discernment tool that you are carrying around with you under your own hat.

Circumstances. The circumstances, which God controls by His divine providence, are an indicator of God's will for you concerning your spouse. You need to develop a skill for reading the circumstances of your romantic relationship to see if this person is God's spouse for you.

Sometimes all the circumstances are perfect, everything just works out, everything seems to fit, to be right. That is easy to read. But what about a situation where the circumstances are not so perfect? Let's say I'm a lawyer in Chicago and have fallen for a med student who lives in New York. If my beloved still has four years of med school, then another four of residency, all in New York, and at the same time my father is dying of cancer and I am his only family and need to care for him here in Chicago, and I am working on a court case that I have worked on for five years that is finally going to trial this year, will take six months to try, and it's worth $1 million in legal fees to me, I should ask myself: from reading these circumstances, what is God trying to say to me? Probably that it is not God's will that I marry this person, at least not right now.

Just because the circumstances are not perfect, however, does not mean someone is not God's will for you. Remember, Satan is the master of this world, and he can throw up lots of circumstantial roadblocks to discourage you and dissuade you from doing God's will in this area.

If all the other signs are pointing to someone as being your spouse but the circumstances are not ideal, go to God with the situation. Ask God that if this is the person He intends for you, that He then make the circumstances work out. Imagine a couple that meets, say, over a Catholic dating Web site, and she lives in Australia and he lives in San Francisco, California. His job is in the U.S. and she does not have that much money for travel or phone calls. But they feel they are called to marriage. Part of discerning if that is really God's will for them is to read the circumstances. Most of us would say, no way, the circumstances seem to say "no." It's too "geographically challenging" of a relationship for it to ever be God's will.

Or is it? What if she quite unexpectedly comes into some money, sufficient to allow a visit to America. Imagine that, quite serendipitously, his company acquires a foreign operation in Australia to which he could apply for a transfer. Imagine that they have access to Internet telephony, so they can "talk" over the Internet every day at no charge. How the circumstances start to fall into place in this manner might be God trying to tell you that this long-distance romance really is His will.

If you are wanting to discern someone and the circumstances surrounding your relationship are not really ideal at present, ask God to make way for the relationship by altering the circumstances, if it is what He wants for you. Whether He answers that prayer, whether the circumstances improve or change in a positive, affirming fashion, should tell you a lot about whether this relationship is the one God has planned for you.

Feelings/Preferences. When it comes to the discernment of feelings, the bottom line is really this: do you love him or her? Are you in love with him or her? Because if you are not, there is nothing to decide about, really. God is not going to yoke you to someone you don't love.

Initially, you have to realize whether you love the person. Pope John Paul II, in his beautiful book *Love and Responsibility*, defines love "as an ambition to ensure the true good of another person" (Wojtyla, p. 272). First, love is a feeling, but then it is also a decision, a commitment. What happens is, you make the decision to *really* love someone, to make all the sacrifices and submissions we saw in Ephesians 5, that decision to lay down your self in loving the person. Love really is a decision, in the end, because the commitment to it is an act of your own will. But it has to start with a feeling. Green says that "feelings are the raw material of discernment" (Green, p. 22). You certainly have to start with whether you feel love for someone for there to be anything further to discern.

Are you maybe only "madly in like" with this person? Do you love being around them, think they are great fun, but don't feel romantic toward them? Do you want to be best buddies with them, but don't really have any desire to be close to them, to kiss them? Then you are not in love. Might it turn into love? Sure, and you need to not be too hasty. But you are in no position to be discerning the vocation of marriage with this person at this point.

Or perhaps are you just infatuated with the idea of this person, rather than being in love with who they really are. Someone extraordinarily beautiful, or blonde, or exotic, or wealthy, or accomplished, might take on some mythical qualities that are not what the person is really about, and that is what you are responding to, not really love

No one else can judge your feelings, but most people would confirm that when you love someone, are in love with someone, you know it. And it might be that in life there will be people you are in love with but who are still not the person that God has called to be your spouse. But be assured, at some point you will be in love with the person that God sends to you as the fulfillment of your call to the vocation of marriage.

Feelings can also manifest themselves as reactions to something, preferences for what you would like. Ask yourself: what do I want to do? What is my own reaction telling me? God has given you a unique set of gifts and talents and desires, and He can speak to you through them. Is this man everything I have ever dreamed of? Do I love everything about him? Could I have not done better myself if I had ordered him up from "central casting"? Hmm, maybe God is trying to tell me something here.

Am I a man whose head is not easily turned, but I find myself totally captivated by this woman, everything she says, everything she does? Does she just astound me every time we talk, every time I see her? Is she the most extraordinary woman I have ever met? Maybe those reactions are God trying to point something out to you.

You need to have the feelings of love in place before you even start to talk about serious discernment. If you don't love, it's not time to discern marriage. Love can grow, and serious discernment about marriage might come later on. If you can't say you are in love yet, but the person for all the other reasons we are looking at still seems to be a good match, a godly match, for you, if there is not some compelling reason not to, you should keep this person in your life, keep getting to know them better. But if, after a reasonable amount of time, you don't feel you love them or are in love, then the right and Christian thing to do is to move on, so you can both find any other persons that God may have in store.

Prayer. Prayer is that profound interaction between us and God. He really wants to hear from you about this most important decision: the selection of your spouse. If you are smart, you have been praying for a long time already that God will lead you to your spouse. You might not always see His hand guiding you along the way, but do believe that He is doing so.

Once you have met someone for whom there is a chance they are your spouse, you really should start praying about this person in particular. You are not now praying with some free-floating intention, "Lord, lead me to my spouse." You now start to pray, "Lord, is Joe my husband?" And God will answer your prayers somehow.

What does God do when you pray to Him about whether this person is your spouse? Does He send you signs, answer you, in a voice, in His Word, through godly advisors, by giving you a consolation, or a knowingness or sense of what He wants for you? Do you feel peace, do you feel relief, do you feel hopeful after praying about it? Do circumstances improve? These kinds of specific prayers about the specific person are very helpful in discerning if they are the spouse God has sent.

You really have to be very focused in prayer at this point. Praying a novena for God to illuminate you on whether this person is your spouse might be an excellent way to show God that you really are seeking His will on this question. You might also go on a retreat alone with the whole point for you being whether this person is your spouse. God loves it when we focus on Him, His voice, and His will.

Another thing you should really do is pray about this person before the Blessed Sacrament. Jesus is right there, and is waiting for you to bring Him all your questions and concerns, including this most important one. The answers or consolations you get while praying before the Blessed Sacrament are good evidence to use in your discernment.

Sometimes one might pray very intently on this specific issue and it seems that God has not answered at all. Sometimes by His silence, God tells us we are doing just what He wants. There is a rule of contract law, on offer and acceptance of contract terms, that says, "Silence constitutes acceptance." Maybe He is well pleased and needs to tell you nothing more. If it seems that God is silent, then look again to the other discernment tools. Might He really be answering you in another area? Or is His silence really acceptance, meaning that He is pleased with what you are doing (dating/knowing this person)? Perhaps His silence tells you that what you are thinking of doing is fine, because surely He would stop you if you were about to make a serious mistake. If God seems silent after specific and continued prayer, and nothing else of the situation points to the opposite, then step out in faith and take the relationship further, and perhaps He will answer you more directly, more profoundly, at a later point in your journey.

Spiritual Direction. It is very important as you progress in your discernment of your spouse that you seek spiritual direction. You are so close to the situation, and in a sense have a vested interest such that you can't be as objective as you need to be. That old expression that love is blind can be very true. You might want the relationship to go one way or the other, and your discernment can get skewed at times, perhaps. That is why a good priest, a good spiritual advisor, is a wonderful resource in discerning your spouse.

Your advisor might, and hopefully does, know your partner. You can just start with getting their opinion—do they think he or she might be the spouse God has sent for you? Share with him what you have gathered in terms of the "raw material" of discernment so far, what you feel Scripture is leading you to, what the Church teaches, answers to prayer, your sense of reason, the circumstances, your feeling, the signs, that point to (or away from) this person as your spouse. A spiritual director in a sense discerns on your discernment. If you share with him what you experience from all the other signs, fruits, feelings, conscience, reason, and answers to prayer, he can test these things in a more objective manner than you might be able to do.

When someone is called to the priesthood, he has a spiritual director to help him discern if he really is called, if he really should be in the seminary. If you are called to the vocation of marriage, you too need to have the help of a godly spiritual advisor to help you and guide you in the very same way.

Ultimately, discernment must be your own, but you need to get input from a godly spiritual director when you are discerning a spouse. This is your vocation we are talking about; it is about the real work and ministry of your life that God had called you to. Choosing the spouse you are called to do it with is the most important choice you will make in your vocation. You *have* to get this right. A priest who knows you and the situation well can be very helpful in your discernment. Don't think that it is too silly or worldly to talk to a priest about your love life. It's your vocation; that is what he is there for, to help you find your way of salvation, and vocation is a part of that journey.

Fruits. Good fruits, bad fruits, consolations, desolations, false consolations—all of these things will show up when you are discerning your spouse. These might be some of the most profound ways you will listen for God's voice about the discernment of your spouse.

If you start dating someone and your whole life starts to fall apart, and lots of bad fruits start coming in, you have to ask yourself: is this someone I should be spending time with? Is there a cause and effect I am supposed to see here? Similarly, if you start dating and everything becomes just grand, good comes in, bad things disappear, you feel joy, peace, and hope, you have to think, wow, where did she come from? Maybe from the hand of God.

As you date someone, however, nothing will always be perfect. But when you are in the relationship, is the balance of the experience good fruits or bad fruits? Generally it will be more one than the other, and that is a great tool for discernment.

You need to be very careful of desolations and false consolations when discerning your spouse. Oftentimes Satan will see that a good thing, something that is God's will, is in the works between the two of you, two people of faith, and so he sends desolations that haunt one or the other of you— things like hurts from the past, areas of pain where growth and healing are still needed, doubts, or shame might come up and begin to sabotage your relationship. If you are with someone and having relationship troubles that stem from these kinds of things, it could well be Satan trying to ruin what God has planned. You really need to examine whether this is a desolation that tells you this person is not the one for you, or whether God is using the desolation to show you both that you need to grow more, be more loving, more forgiving, more truthful, more charitable to each other, in order to take yourselves into the vocation of marriage together.

Similarly, you have to be very careful about false consolations. As we saw in Chapter 3, Satan uses those more with more devout souls because they are all the more confusing. Here's an example. Let's say that you have been very upset about whether a particular woman is the one for you, really struggling about it, and praying about her, and you decide, no, I think there is still someone better out there for me, and you cut her off and break up. And then you think you feel a sense of peace.

There is a saying, that "peacefulness follows any decision, even the wrong one" (Rita Mae Brown). Of course you will feel "peace," or at least relief, just to have made the decision and not be tormented by the question any longer. But that "peace" might just be in having done something—anything—about the situation. Or that "peace" could also be that Satan, having now influenced you to make the wrong move, is not going to bother you for a while, and the absence of his torment is what you are interpreting as peace. Look out for things like that. Christ's peace is consistent over time.

Or maybe you meet someone and you are just so happy to be dating, to not be alone, to have something to do on Saturday nights, that you take that as a consolation from God that this is the person for you. That could also be a false consolation from the devil—his way of luring you into a relationship that is going to occupy your time, and keep you from the one that God really has in mind for you, just because you are feeling lonely or desperate. Watch out for that as well.

You might ask how Satan could have any place in the relationship between two devout, seeking Catholics thinking about the sacrament of marriage. Don't be lulled into thinking that is not precisely a place where Satan feels he can do his best work. St. John of the Cross noted that the devil will work much harder to ruin and deflect even one committed soul (let alone two) than to harm a greater number of less committed souls (*Living Flame of Love*, Stanza III, no. 64).

Satan can get two for the price of one, in a sense, if he defeats God's will when it comes to mis-discerning the call to the vocation of marriage. He not only gets the two of you off the right track but he also stops your children from being born. So to interfere with God's chosen spouse for you is something that packs a lot of punch for Satan. Why wouldn't he want to interfere with it?

So you need to gird yourself for his assaults when it comes to discerning your spouse. We never said that this process was going to be all sweet and nice just because it's about love and God, and this is an example of that. Satan would like nothing more than to keep you from your spouse, and he will do everything he can to do that. Don't forget that.

Eventually, what you are looking for with fruits and consolations is their enduring nature and quality. If there are long-term good fruits to your relationship, that is a confirming sign that God is pleased that you are in that relationship. Fruits like peace, an increase in faith, increase in devotion, increase in practices, increase in wisdom and understanding, patience, kindness, self-giving, are all good fruits and consolations that would be the signs that God has His Hand on the relationship. If, over time, that is not what you are experiencing for the most part, or experiencing overall, then you need to seriously consider whether this can be God's spouse for you.

Jesus said you will know a thing by its fruits (Matt. 7:16, 20; 12:33). So judge your relationship in that manner, and God will not disappoint you.

Signs. Signs and wonders, as in all discernment, are best left to the end, and are best used as confirmations of a larger discernment, not as the whole of discernment. That is as true in discernment in general as it is for discernment of your spouse.

You often hear stories that someone prayed, "God, let the next woman who walks into the dance be my wife," and, lo and behold, it was, and he married her. You should not test God like that. It makes for a good story, and a "sign" might be part of your discernment story someday, but don't hang your hat on a sign alone when it comes to discerning a spouse.

When people are confused and sincerely seeking an answer about something, they are quick to see signs in everything. Say you have a boyfriend and you are wondering if he is "the one," and it comes up in conversation that someone has his same birthday. Is that a sign from God that he is your husband, or just a coincidence? You have to test that.

Should you seek signs as to who is your spouse? There are two schools of thought on that. The Bible says, don't put the Lord your God to the test (Deut. 6:16; Luke 4:12). But it also says, ask and you shall receive (Matt. 7:7).

The answer probably is that you should not test the Lord in grave matters just to see if He will come through—for example, don't jump off a building to see if God will save you if you ask Him to. That is putting God to the test in a foolish manner.

But He does want you to come to Him. If you are getting down to a final discernment about someone for marriage, there is nothing wrong with asking Him to give you a clear sign which way you are to go. Ask Him, "Lord, please send me a clear sign; is Karen my wife, or not?"

When dealing with signs, you need to pray about them silently. Satan and his minions are listening to every word you say and plotting your ruin from those observations, so pray for a sign privately in your heart. That way it's just between you and God. Don't talk about your request for a sign, because other people might interfere with it, even if they are trying to be helpful. It's best not to limit God on what the sign is to be. Pray that He send a sign that you will understand, that will be clear to you. That should be sufficient. He will send you an answer, and maybe it will be in the form of a sign that you will understand.

In a matter of such importance, if you have discerned all the other indicia of God's will and are at a critical juncture, trying to make a final discernment, asking for a sign is a good thing to do. God doesn't want you to make a mistake in this.

Some signs will just happen to you even without asking for them, but you have to be ready to see them and be open to what they might mean. Here's an example. Let's say you are with your partner with whom you are discerning deeply about marriage, and while you are out together, you keep running into weddings. You go to a Saturday evening Mass together and you see a bride and groom getting showered with rice on the church steps. A wedding party's caravan goes honking past you in traffic. You are at a hotel restaurant for dinner and you encounter a wedding party assembling in the garden gazebo for photographs. You take a dinner cruise and you see a wedding taking place on a passing yacht. You are at the ball game and some guy asks his girlfriend to marry him with a proposal emblazoned on the scoreboard. And you don't seem to ever see wedding stuff on your own, but only when you are with this person. Is that a sign this person is your spouse? Could be. It's not a sign you asked for, but if you are looking with the eyes of faith, you recognize that it could be God talking to you.

Some signs might be very subject to interpretation. Say you purchased a particular rosary, and when you bought it, you called it your wedding rosary; you wanted to carry it on your wedding day because it's got pretty pearl beads. And say that you then began praying the rosary every day with those wedding rosary beads for the intention of your future marriage and your spouse. And say that you mislaid the rosary and it's lost now, even after months of searching for it. Then it very unexpectedly reappears when you are dating a particular person whom you are really feeling good things about. Is that a sign from God that your prayers through the intercession of the Blessed Mother for your marriage and spouse are answered in your present partner? Or is it only a sign that you need to be a better, more thorough housekeeper? You will have to discern which it is.

Many Catholics have a great devotion to St. Thérèse of Lisieux, and there is a rich tradition in the Church of praying for her intercession. There is a well-known novena by which you pray to St. Thérèse for your intention and ask her, if the intention is God's will, if it will come to pass, that she send you a rose from an unexpected source. If you pray such a novena, asking for St. Thérèse's intercession on whether your partner is your spouse, and you "miraculously" get a rose in a manner you don't expect or seek out (such as, your partner who has never given you flowers through the courtship now brings you roses, or you literally find a rose in your path as you are walking), is that a sign from God that your prayer is answered "yes"?

You will have to judge the circumstances of the sign yourself, and should do so carefully with your spiritual director. But keep your eyes and ears open for such signs, and then test them. They might be God's voice, or His Hand, in your situation.

You might get a real answer to prayer, like a locution or a vision. These things cannot be ruled out. If you pray, "Is Susan my wife?" and God intones in your ear, "Yes, my son, she is," that would be a very profound experience. But you would have to be very circumspect about such an experience, checking it out with your spiritual director before you run out and buy an engagement ring for Susan based on that. The fruits of such an extraordinary experience have to be weighed and judged themselves before you can see where it might fit into the larger discernment about marriage.

The bottom line is, signs are nice, and they can be very comforting, and they can be a way in which God gives a confirmation to discernment that is already taking place about a person as your spouse. But they should not be used as the be-all and end-all of discernment when it comes to marriage or anything else. You should be open to them, but you need to test any signs that come into your life, whether it's a sign you asked for or one that comes unexpectedly.

Conclusion. The Lord has a will for your life, including for the selection of your spouse. As with all life decisions, you need to discern what that will is for you. You do this by collecting data and evidence through Scripture, Church teaching, feelings, prayer, reason, conscience, the circumstances, spiritual direction, fruits, and signs. As in all discernment, God will speak to your heart in these ways, if you are listening, and will give you a very good idea of whether someone is His chosen spouse for you. Discernment is about helping you make a sound and educated decision. There is no way to know absolutely for sure what God's will is about anything, and that certainly includes the identity of your future spouse. But all these aspects of discernment will help you collect data, and are essential to making such an important decision with good judgment.

Chapter 5

Great Expectations: What God Generally Will and Won't Do

Discernment is figuring out what God's will is for you in a particular situation. The particular situation we are concerned with is deciding with whom God means for you to serve Him in the vocation of marriage. Discernment means observing, recognizing, and responding to the movements of God's presence in your life as it concerns this most important decision. It means seeing what is going on around you, hearing what is being said to you, analyzing what is happening to you and what is going on inside your heart. All of these things can be God speaking to you about who it is He means for you to marry.

How do you know, though, what thoughts, feelings, insights, and signs are more likely from God as opposed to some other source (your own thoughts, others' influences, or even Satan's interference)? That is what the consolations and desolations are for, but frankly that is the hardest part of discernment. So it might help to know that there are some things that God is more likely to do and some things that He more likely will not do.

You can be sure that everything that comes to you about your discernment will claim to be God's doing, claim to be His voice, and claim to be from Him, even if it's not. Part of your job of discernment—all discernment, but particularly here since we are talking about discerning the vocation of marriage—is to figure out what insights and signs on this important question are actually coming from God and which are coming from some other source, masquerading as God.

There are certain types of things that can happen to you as you seek an answer to the question "Lord, what would you have me do? Lead me in the call to the vocation of marriage." You might have feelings, answers to prayer, insights from Scripture readings, people saying things to you that speak to your heart on the subject, or even visions, signs, or inner locutions, or actually "hear" God speak to you on this topic. But not all of them will be from God. They all will claim to be, and you will sincerely want and hope for them all to be, because you are earnestly seeking His will. But you have to carefully figure out what is more likely from the Lord and thus should be accepted and followed, and what is more likely than not to be from a source that is not the Lord, either your own imagination, other people's influences or actions, or even from a dark influence, from Satan, and should therefore be rejected, or at the very least considered with great skepticism and awarded less weight in your discernment.

Let's first look at what kind of things are more likely *not* going to be from God, what God generally would *not* do.

First, **God will not** give you total clarity and 100 percent certainty about who it is you should marry. Wouldn't that be nice if He would? He will lead you very specifically to a person with whom He wants you to discern the vocation of marriage. He will allow you to have experiences that bring you to the conclusion that a certain person is meant to be your spouse, and take you to a level of moral certainty about it, which is what you must and should have before going forward with a commitment as important as marriage. But if you are thinking that unless you are 100 percent sure about someone, then they can't be "the one," you need to rethink that. Similarly, if you are absolutely, positively, no question about it, 100 percent sure someone is your spouse, that should give you pause as well.

Why? Because God reveals His will to you in bits and starts, without revealing the whole picture. He does this so that you will walk in faith with Him, so that you have to trust in Him and not in yourself, or in how smart you think you are, or in how insightful you think you are. You are to walk in faith when it comes to discerning the vocation of marriage, at least in part. The only one who can know everything and understand everything perfectly is God Himself, and the only thing that we can be 100 percent sure of in this life is the dogmas of the Church, the tenets of our faith. We are always going to be at least a little bit in the dark about everything else, including the call to marriage.

You hear people say that marriage requires a leap of faith. And even when you have really focused and tried really hard to discern God's will for you on this question, in the end you probably are going to have to step out in faith, at least a little bit. You discern as long as you can, and as best as you can, and then you draw a conclusion. If the conclusion is that you are to marry a certain person, then you step out in faith and you ask her to marry you, or you accept his proposal. And it is often afterward that your faith is rewarded, that you feel more sure and know somehow that it feels more right, now that you have acted on the discernment and the decision.

If they are honest, most people, Catholic and non-Catholic, admit that they still feel a little doubt even as they prepare for their wedding day—not serious doubts, but maybe a little nagging: am I really doing the right thing? And this is not only normal, it's a good thing, because it means you are still keeping your heart open to hear God's will, seeking to know more and more if you are doing the right thing, what He wants you to do with your life, and being open to Him correcting you if you are wrong somehow.

So God will probably not ever give you total certainty concerning who it is you are meant to marry in His perfect plan. But He will be there with you when you make such a monumental decision in your life, if you stay close to Him and keep praying with an open heart.

Second, **God will not** drag you into the vocation of marriage. He is not the Lord of involuntary servitude. He won't make you serve Him in marriage at all, and He won't make you serve with a person that you don't also choose. He will put a call on your heart for what He wants most from you if you are to serve Him in the vocation of marriage. He will lead you to the person that He wants you to serve, and in serving them, thereby serve and glorify Him. He will see to it that the person comes into your life. But once He brings him or her to you, He will let you choose and decide. If you feel you are stuck with someone, or have no better prospects, know that God will not impose marriage or a particular spouse on you.

Third, **God won't** call you to the vocation of marriage and then not give you the opportunity for the fulfillment of that vocation. If you are called, He will see to it that the person with whom you are called to the vocation comes into your life. Whether you discern properly and recognize who the person is meant to be to you is your job. What you discern to do about the person is up to you, and similarly, what the other person discerns to do with you is also up to them. God has given us all free will. But be assured that if He has called you, He will bring the opportunity for the fulfillment of the vocational call to you. Whatever the circumstances look like, trust in that.

Another thing that **God is not likely to do** is to tell you exact details about your spouse, like their name, their physical appearance, or about your wedding, the number of children you will have someday, or other highly factual information about your future or your future spouse. Remember, an evil spirit's movements lead to "useless things, curious things, impertinent things" (Most, *Discernment of Spirits*). God is not a fortuneteller or a psychic. While He is omniscient, and knows your future, He does not reveal that future to you just for the fun of it.

For example, say you are praying and are asking that God reveal your wife to you; you are really seeking to know whom you are looking for. You are praying this prayer when you are not even dating anyone, which is a fine thing to do. But if a woman's name then suddenly comes to you, pops into your mind, sorry to say it, but that insight is most likely not from God.

Why? God would never limit your gift of free will in that manner. If the name "Kathy" comes to you as you are praying for a wife, that is not necessarily God telling you that some girl named Kathy is your wife. Why? Because it is simply human nature that you then would seriously look at only women named Kathy, and anyone whose name is not Kathy you are probably going to look past, if you believed your insight was really from God. God would never limit your free will to choose your own spouse in this manner. No, more likely than not, these kinds of factual predictions of the future are either from your own imagination or from Satan and his dark, interfering influences, and not from God.

Such an experience has Satan's signature written all over it. Just because something comes to you while you are praying does not mean that it could only be from God. Satan and his minions are watching you all the time; they can see you are praying, they know you are desperately seeking answers. They observe you and see what is troubling you, they know what stage or juncture you are at in your life, they know what you are talking about to your friends, what you are writing about in your journal, what books you are reading. They are very cunning and good at figuring out what is on your mind and about what you might be praying.

The act of prayer does not put some impenetrable bubble of protection around you so that you can't be influenced by or have an experience that is from Satan, just because you are in the midst of praying. Always remember, Satan can get to you anywhere, as long as you are on this planet, so until you are in heaven, you have to assume his influences are around you, even intruding upon your thoughts and insights that come while praying.

Anyone whose mind has wandered to unholy or unchaste thoughts while at Mass knows that this is true. Satan can influence you anywhere, at any time, even when you are praying. So just because something seems to be an "answer" to the act of praying to God does not make it so. It is not necessarily a cause and effect situation. "I prayed x and then y was in my mind, so that means it was God's answer to my prayer." That is not necessarily the case.

Also, God will not reveal things to you that are not pertinent or germane for you to know. He won't tell you something to satisfy your curiosity or "just for fun." It would be kind of fun to think you know whom you are marrying in advance. It's like a parlor game: you get to see if it comes true. But in actuality, continuing with that last example, there is no reason for God to tell you your spouse's name before you have even met this person. Such information is of no real importance or meaning for you at the time. This is because you are really on a "need to know" basis when it comes to God's will, and these kinds of facts are not something you need to know yet.

Further, God would never take away your free will like that. It is up to you whom you marry. So if you think God has revealed detailed information to you about something like that into the future, you had better discern on that again, because it is more likely Satan trying to trick you.

Why would Satan do this—give you an insight that you think is from God when it's really from him? That is easy: to keep you from finding and following God's real will for your life. Just think about it. If you believed that "detailed insight," let's call it, is the truth about your future, and let's say God's *real* will for you is to marry a woman that He has prepared for you named Mary (not Kathy), you might meet your Mary, but because she is not named Kathy, she doesn't register with you, and you then miss your opportunity with her because you were focusing on the hunt for Kathy. See how Satan has just caused you to defeat God's perfect will for your life, and you just missed out on the real woman of your dreams?

Also, just think about how you are going to feel when no Kathy comes along. Talk about desolation! How upsetting will it be for you when what you thought for some time was going to be "God's will" for you does not come to pass. Satan loves to set you up for that and then pull the rug out from under you, because what he hopes is that you will then turn on God, and blame God, and lose your faith in Him because you thought that plan was coming from Him. "Hey, Lord, I thought I was going to marry a woman named Kathy by now. Why did you take that away from me? What did I do wrong? Why are you persecuting me like this? Why did You mislead me? Why am I so bad at discerning Your will after all this time? I might as well just give up on this marriage business and everything else. I am hopeless." Satan wants to do anything he can to drive a wedge between you and the Lord. And what better place to do it than in this most important issue of your life—your search and holy desire for a godly spouse? Never underestimate Satan's ability to influence your thoughts.

So be very wary of any factually specific "insights" that come your way. St. Augustine warned about such things. Before his conversion, while he was still living a life of great debauchery, wild partying, and sexual sinning, his mother,

St. Monica, would pray earnestly that he get married, thinking that would settle him down. At one point she even thought the Lord had revealed details to her about his upcoming marriage. Augustine wrote:

> At which time, verily, both at my request and her own desire, with strong heartfelt cries did we daily beg of Thee that Thou wouldest by a vision disclose unto her something concerning my future marriage; but Thou wouldest not. She saw indeed certain vain and fantastic things, such as the earnestness of a human spirit, bent thereon, conjured up; and these she told me of, not with her usual confidence when Thou hadst shown her anything, but slighting them. For she could, she declared, through some feeling which she could not express in words, discern the difference betwixt Thy revelations and the dreams of her own spirit. (Augustine, *Confessions,* Chap. XIII, 23)

Well, we all know that St. Augustine didn't marry, so that "detailed insight" of St. Monica's was not from God. But if St. Monica could be influenced by Satan like that (in her own fanciful imaginings), so can you. What God really had in mind for her son was not to be a married man but that he become one of the greatest saints the Church has known. She just wanted him to settle down and marry a nice girl, and thought she knew "detailed insights" about that marriage. If she was a saint and was completely wrong about that, if she could be misled, so can you. God did not reveal to St. Monica future factual details just to make her feel better, and He will probably not do that for you either.

On the other hand, if you are in serious discernment, or are trying to discern between two persons as potential spouses such that your questions to God have a context, it's not way off in the future but the issue is actually joined in your life, there is a decision that has to be made between these two, and one of their names keeps coming to you, that might be God trying to lead your heart, if He has brought one of these persons to you to be your spouse. Do you see how different that is from the earlier example? He is not taking away your free will here. You are free to choose either one, but in this example He is tugging at your heart, one way or the other, because you are seeking Him. In the earlier example, it would be as if He has predestined you— programmed you like a robot—for Kathy. That is not free will, and God would never take your free will away from you like that.

Another example of things that are **more likely not from God** is dreams. Dreams that occur when you are sleeping are most probably not visions from God but rather your own subconscious, your own confused feelings and desires expressing themselves naturally while you sleep. As you discern whether you are called to marriage with a particular person, if you have a dream that the two of you are getting married, and you dream about that wedding, you would of course want to consider that occurrence. You would want to note and ponder what the dream showed and, more importantly, how you feel about what you dreamed, but you probably should not jump to the conclusion that the dream was God telling you that you are supposed to marry that person.

Why? Because it is natural that if you are thinking a lot about marriage while you are awake, and you are spending a lot of time with your boyfriend/girlfriend in your waking hours, your subconscious mind would string these two subjects together into a dream about a wedding between the two of you. That does not mean the dream was sent from God.

Now the Bible does reveal that God has spoken to some of his faithful people in dreams or visions, and therefore it *could* happen, but what you need to be mindful of is that

God does not talk to most people in this manner most of the time. And everybody dreams every night, and not every dream is a message from God, that is for sure. You need only think about some of your own crazy and wild mixed-up dream story lines to know that is true.

But how you feel after the dream is another matter. Do you feel happy and excited about this dream of possibly marrying your current love? Now those feelings are good information on which you can do some serious discernment. On the other hand, does the wedding dream make you feel uneasy, nervous, and scared somehow, as if it were a nightmare? That is also good information for discernment. So while the dream is not necessarily a message from God as to whom you are meant to marry, your thoughts and emotions about the dream might well be His influence, speaking to your heart about that subject which the dream brought to the surface.

Those are some overriding concepts of things that God most likely won't do in this process. If you ever feel that God has told you something 100 percent, or that He is imposing something or someone on you, or that He's not sending you someone, or that He's not fulfilling your vocation, or that He is giving you specific future details or marching orders or feature film-length premonitions, you're probably not discerning something properly.

If those are some of the things that God most likely will not do to you in your search for a spouse, then what **will God do**? What is more likely to be revealed as God's hand in your discernment?

The most important thing to be assured of is that if you are indeed called to the vocation of marriage, **God will** send you the person with whom He intends for you to live out that vocation. Absolutely, if you are called, He will send the person. You can rest assured of that.

If you feel you are called, and the person is not showing up at this point, it means one of three things: (1) you have not discerned the general call to the vocation of marriage correctly, and in fact you are actually called to the religious life or the celibate single life, and the reason the person is not showing up is that you are in the wrong vocation; no one is going to show because you are actually called elsewhere; (2) the person already came into your life, and your exercise of your free will has kept the person from you, or the person is in your life now, and you just don't recognize him or her as of yet; or (3) the person is yet to appear in your life. Always remember that what you do when God presents the person to you is what this discernment journey is really all about.

What else will God do for you in your search? Since God does want us to know His will for our lives, **God will** answer your prayers about your call to the vocation of marriage. Exactly how He will answer those prayers can be in many different ways and through many different means, as we have seen, but He will answer your prayers and guide you somehow if you really seek for Him to do so. He delights in doing so. Sometimes His answer to your prayers is that He changes your heart. If He changes your heart, then what you ask for changes too, and that is His answer. He makes you want something different. But He does answer.

Another thing you can be assured of that God will do for you is **God will** always let you choose your spouse. He will never take your free will from you. He will let you choose the person you want, even if it is not the person He wants for you. That is the reason that He created you—to allow you to choose and do what you want to do. That is what He would have you do, but He will never impose that on you. He delights in revealing His will to us, and then in seeing what we do with that knowledge. And He is delighted when we choose what He would have us do. But He will let you choose.

God will do something else. **He will** send someone to serve you in the vocation of marriage whose love for you is a reflection of His love for you—that "agape" love; some-one who loves you unconditionally, someone who loves you just as you are, the whole of who you are, someone for whom you don't have to be anything special or different for them to love you. He will send you someone who cares about you more than they do themselves. He will send you someone who wants your good more than their own. He will send someone who is willing to sacrifice their comfort and their needs and their desires for yours. If you ever meet anyone who loves you like that, you would do well to give that person your serious discernment.

God will also give you all the grace and wisdom you need for this journey. It's in His best interest to do so. If He wants us to find a spouse, marry, and have and raise up children in the faith, to His glory, who will serve and glorify Him for generations to come, it's in His best interest to see that you have everything you need to walk this path. So don't have any fears that you are not up to this important task, or that it's all too complicated and that it shouldn't be this hard. This is the most important decision you will ever make, if you are indeed called to the married vocation. This is the beginning of the real work of your life—to recognize your spouse, the partner suitable for you in your vocational service to God. This is certainly a time when you simply have to get everything right. Because it is so very impor-tant, God is not going to deny you the tools you need to do that.

He is going to see to it that you educate yourself about this, such as by reading this book and others on discerning His will. He is going to see to it that you read and learn about the faith and its teachings, and about marriage in gen-eral, so you can know exactly what you are getting into and what you are looking for. He is going to send you godly advisors—your parents, other married Catholics, priests and spiritual advisors, and friends, married and single, who are going to help you in this walk. And he is going to send you dates and suitors who will teach you much about yourself and love along the way, so you can know your spouse when God brings him or her to you. And ultimately He is going to send that person who is to be your spouse, and through him or her, He will really give you the grace you need to experience your "exclamation." He is going to be with you Himself in this most important task of your life because He wants what is best for you and is going to help you find it for yourself.

Another thing you can depend on is that **God will** send you the right person, the partner that is suitable for you, just as He did for Adam, if you are really seeking His will in the call. What you think is perfect for you and what He thinks is perfect and suitable for you might be exactly the same thing, as if God sent you the person out of "central casting"—as if you could not have done better in casting the role of your spouse than if you had created him yourself. On the other hand, it may take God speaking to your heart for a while to show you that the person He has selected is in fact perfect for you, even if she is, say, a brunette (because you always thought you wanted a blonde). Either way, you can be assured that the person God ultimately brings for you will be the person that will best serve you, and that you can best serve, and with whom you both in turn can best serve God together in the vocation of marriage. That is the perfect person for you, and God will send that person to you, be assured.

Never forget God's words for you, from the prophet Jeremiah: "For I know the plans I have for you, says the LORD, plans for welfare and not for evil, to give you a future and a hope" (Jer. 29:11). God knows what He is doing. Be open to seeing what He is doing, and not doing, and put all your trust in Him.

Chapter 6

Catholic "Speed Dating":
Ten Shortcuts to Discernment

Couples often make the mistake of spending a lot of time going to movies, out to dinner, and hanging out with friends, and think that discernment as to whether each person is "the one" for the other will just alight upon them at some moment, like the bluebird of happiness. They think that maybe someday they will look at each other over a drink or in a group of friends at the game, and just get hit by the lightning bolt that tells them, yes, this is the man or woman for me. That might happen, but for the seeking Catholic, there are some more effective and faster catalysts or ways in which to bring to the surface the answer of whether this person might be God's partner for you. There actually are some shortcuts to seeing whether you might have or are likely to find "the exclamation" for the person you are dating.

When you are looking for your spouse and waiting for that confirmation from heaven to hit you, it seems there is little you can do to help the process along. Nothing is further from the truth. There is plenty you can do, and do early on so as not to waste time with someone who is not God's planned partner for you.

The Catholic faith, tradition, and culture offer many opportunities for discernment. Here is a helpful list of ten things you can do to hasten the discernment of whether someone is your spouse. To some extent, these techniques might be ways to do what can be called "negative discernment"—figuring out that which is *not* God's will for you, that someone is *not* the right person for you. This is helpful because you might be able to discern early on, faster, and therefore not waste time and opportunity in a dating relationship that is not the right one for you. Some of these suggestions are not uniquely Catholic, but some really are. So let's turn to them and see how you can speed along your discernment of your holy spouse while dating.

1. Pray together. A Catholic marriage's base foundation is prayer: prayer for one another, prayer for your marriage, prayer for your children, prayer for your place in serving the Catholic community and the world at large. Prayer is the bedrock of a good, solid marriage. Ask most married couples if they pray together and you might get a lot of blank stares and laughs, but truly, without prayer, a marriage stands little chance of surviving in this toxic world, which does all it can to destroy this sacramental and societal institution.

And besides, you don't want a marriage that is of this world anyway, but rather one where God is its heart and center. Be assured that the gift of praying together does not just start magically on the day you get married. Rather, a foundation of prayer must begin long, long before the wedding day, or there is not much chance that the marriage will be based on the habit, routine, and grace of prayer.

Once you are in a relationship with a person you are discerning, prayer should be a part of it from the start. This is not as hard as it might sound. First, you might have already met the person in a church prayer group or a Catholic singles group, and you might have the chance for prayer together first as part of that group. That will make it all the more natural for the two of you to start praying on your own together.

But here's a great starter idea—begin praying together on your very first date. Most first dates are dinner and a movie, right? Food is generally involved on a date in some way, shape, or form. What do Catholics do before we eat? We pray grace. Let the first meal you have together on your first date, the first time you break bread together, begin with praying grace together.

You might think that praying on a first date might be weird or awkward, particularly in a restaurant. Put that kind of thinking aside. First, to suggest you pray grace together shows right away that you are living your Catholic faith, be it in private or out in public. It shows that you are willing to witness to your faith, even on a first date with someone you don't know all that well. It also shows that you want to get this relationship off on the right foot from the start, with a focus on faith, prayer, and thanksgiving to God, and not just on whether he looks cute in that blue sweater, or whether you are going to make the 8:00 movie on time if you order the dessert.

So when the first course comes, simply say, "Is it your custom to say grace before you eat?" That's simple—it's a question, it's not judgmental, and while it does not press the issue, it's an invitation to pray with you. If he or she says "yes," simply smile (because this is good news to you—a person who actually prays, thanks be to God) and just say, "Would you like to lead us or shall I?" Then bow your head and pray your first prayer together. What a beautiful thing, to pray together.

Once you are past that first time of praying together, it gets easier. You can start a habit of praying together on your dinner dates. It just happens, really. The food is served and you both automatically bow your heads, maybe hold hands, and quietly pray grace.

You might then start a routine of praying a short prayer together when you part after a date, or when you are about to get off the phone if you are talking at night. Simply suggest, "Well, I'd better say good night now, but would you like to say a Hail Mary together before we go?" It is so easy, so short, so almost inconsequential, but you will see that the prayer bond between you will grow and grow, and start to form a foundation of prayer that you need if you are hoping to see if this is the person who will be your spouse.

You would be surprised how quickly you come into the habit of this; if you forget to suggest it, your significant other will say, "Oh, we almost forgot to pray." And then you will really know that you are forming a good habit together that will not fail you if you are called to the vocation of marriage together.

As you mature as a couple, you might start praying together for special intentions. "Let's say the Chaplet of Divine Mercy together for your sick uncle" or "Can we say a prayer about my big exam tomorrow? I am really nervous about it." That way the prayer becomes more spontaneous, more interactive, coming more deeply from each of your hearts.

If you are well on your way to discernment about each other, a more intensive prayer life together should be forming, such as praying the rosary together on Sundays or praying a novena together for some intention the two of you have. The Church's treasury and tradition of prayer are rich with opportunity for the two of you to grow together in prayer, and you should use the prayers and devotions that speak to you as individuals and as a couple.

The discernment that comes from praying together can't be underestimated. For example, what of the person who does not want to pray with you? What about someone who is embarrassed to even pray grace at a restaurant with you? You have to ask yourself, what kind of a Catholic and Christian witness will our family be to the world if he doesn't want to be a witness to our faith now, in such a small way?

Or what if she will pray with you, but isn't really interested in it? Sure, she will pray if you ask, but she doesn't seek it or see it as an important part of the relationship. That should speak volumes to you about whether this woman is the spouse God has sent for you.

Sometimes one person is more comfortable than the other with communal prayer, and that is understandable, as everyone has a different religious history and tradition, and maybe you are there to be a good influence on him or her, and they will come along, and you should give that a chance. But if, after some time, your friend is not showing progress on the habit of praying together, it's time to seriously consider whether he or she can be God's intended for you.

2. Go to Mass together. The greatest prayer we have is the Mass. We are so blessed to be part of the faith given to us by Christ himself, handed down through Peter and the apostles, and that we can come together to the Lord's table and commune with Him, Body and Blood, Soul and Divinity. What better prayer to pray together than attending Mass with the person you are testing to see if they are your spouse?

The opportunities to attend Mass are plentiful. If you are going out on a date on Saturday night, why not start it with the 5 p.m. Mass first? If you are going to get together for an outing on Sunday afternoon, why not start off with 11 a.m. Mass? If you are both going to Mass anyway, why not start going together as soon as you can?

Or what about attending Mass after a date? What about spending the day together and then attending an early-evening Mass? Knowing that you are going to receive the Lord in the Eucharist at the end of a date is also a good way to ensure that your time together will be completely chaste (see Chapter 9).

Attendance at Sunday Mass is the most basic requirement in practicing the Catholic faith. And it is the one place you often hear married couples start slacking off in the practice of the faith. "Oh, we didn't go to Mass because we were out of town." "Oh, the football game was on and we were having people over." You want to find out early on if this person's priority is attendance at Mass and fulfillment of their Sunday obligation, or if they are really not that firm and committed to it.

You can also learn a lot about a person by going to Mass with them. It's not hard to suggest, because it's an activity. You just suggest it. "Hey, how about we go to Mass at St. Mary's beforehand? They have an 11:00 Mass." It's as easy as that. Sometimes suggesting going to Mass together is even easier than suggesting you pray together, because Mass is not so interactive but is an activity, there is a lot going on, and you don't have to always be "on," thinking up things to talk about. Really, it's kind of like going to the movies on those early dates—you are together, you get to sit next to each other, and even if you are not directly interacting, you can make lots of observations that are very telling.

You can find out so many things about someone, and their faith, at Mass. Do they really know their faith or are they haltingly going through the motions? Do they know when to stand and sit and kneel? Do they know the prayers and responses by heart? Do they really listen to and read along with the Liturgy of the Word or do they zone out? Do they have a reverence for this holy place and can you see it in how they act in church? Do they sing the hymns, whether they have a good singing voice or not? (That's always a good sign).

Are they focused on the celebration of the Mass or are they reading the bulletin? Are they devout and humble at the consecration or are they looking around at the people? Do they reverently receive the Lord in the Eucharist? Do they receive under both species, or do they think the Cup is "too germy"? Are they kind and friendly to those around you at the "kiss of peace"? Do they greet the priest or shake his hand as you exit?

It's terribly important to get to Mass together as soon as you can with a new friend, and who knows, you might even get a sweet kiss or hug at the sign of peace!

In all seriousness, if someone does not want to go to Mass with you, that should be a huge warning sign. If someone always has an excuse about why you can't go to Mass together, flashing red lights should be going off as to whether this is the person God has selected for you. If every time you suggest Mass, he or she says, "Oh, we don't have time" or "I forgot to find out the Mass schedule" or "I'm too tired to go to Mass now" or "We'll miss the start of the football game," that should speak volumes about how he or she sees this most elemental part of the practice of our faith, and where he or she sees its place in your relationship too.

But let's say you two are able to go to Mass together, and it's going along well. As your relationship progresses, you might even form the habit of going to weekday Mass together. Maybe start small, with Saturday daytime Mass. Or start with Mass on Friday night after you both get off work but before your Friday-night date. Going to an "extra" Mass that is your own special time together can be very telling of where your relationship is meant to go.

There is a lovely young engaged couple that I see at 5:00 daily Mass. He is always there early, praying. She must not get off until 5:00, because she always slips into the pew next to him during the Liturgy of the Word. They hold hands and very devoutly celebrate Mass together after their working day. After Mass, they stay and pray together, on their knees, side by side. Now that is a couple who is making the practice of the faith part of their relationship, and providing an example for us all.

Scripture says that after the Resurrection the apostles recognized Jesus "in the breaking of the bread" (See Chapter 7). Just like the disciples, by attending Mass with someone you are discerning may be your God-given spouse, you have a better chance of recognizing him or her as you share Christ in the Eucharist at Mass.

3. Adore the Blessed Sacrament together. If Christ is to be the center of your marriage, and Christ is truly present in the Blessed Sacrament, what better place to first invite Him into your relationship than before Him at the tabernacle? Attendance at a Holy Hour with exposition of the Blessed Sacrament, or silent adoration in the adoration chapel (if you are lucky enough to have a parish nearby that has regular or perpetual adoration), is a wonderful way to ask Christ into your relationship and listen to what He speaks to your heart about the two of you.

Eucharistic adoration is one place you are assured that Christ is present, ready and waiting to speak to you. It's kind of like how you bring someone home to meet your parents (see below). You need to take someone you are interested in before the Lord, and present yourselves to Him as a couple, and begin to find out if He "approves" of your being together.

Eucharistic adoration fell "out of fashion" in many parishes after Vatican Council II, but it is one of the greatest treasures of our faith. It is now again being celebrated more and more often, at Catholic conferences, on First Fridays, on Holy Thursday, and in perpetual adoration chapels, and participating in it can be a valuable tool in the discernment of a marriage partner.

Why? Because Christ is truly present in the Eucharist. Where He is is holy ground. There is peace where He is. Fewer distractions. Dark influences generally are left at the door of the adoration chapel. It's quiet and reverent. What better place to discern on the most important question of your life?

Starting in on this might be a little more difficult than Mass or prayer. This might be something that you do after you have been dating for a time. If one of you is not used to adoration, you might suggest a little reading, or you may have some explaining to do on the practice and about why it is so efficacious to go before the Lord in the Blessed Sacrament.

That process alone might tell you something that you really need to know: that your "Catholic" friend does not believe in the Real Presence of Jesus in the Blessed Sacrament, and if that is the case, she would not be God's intended spouse for you. To be in communion with the Church, one must believe in all the dogmas, and belief that the Eucharist is truly the Body of Christ is a tenet of the faith that a Catholic must believe and accept. If she doesn't see the point of going and sitting "with a piece of bread" for an hour, then she is probably not your Catholic wife. And it is a sorry thing to have to say that you may well find more than a few people who consider themselves Catholic but don't actually believe in the Eucharist. You can try to encourage them, and "instruct the ignorant" (that is one of the spiritual acts of mercy, after all), but unless and until they believe in the True Presence, they are not God's Catholic spouse for you.

But if you find out that your Catholic friend is a true believer in the Real Presence, and if you are fortunate enough to have perpetual adoration at a church in your area, you and your friend can stop in anytime, before, during, or after a date. What a wonderful thing, to make Christ in the Eucharist a part of your times together. Like attending Mass, adoring Christ together is not necessarily all that interactive, because you have to be silent, but again, you can learn so much about someone just by being with them before the Lord.

But even more so, it is your opportunity to really, physically place your friend before the Lord, and ask the Lord to speak to *your* heart about him, about whether this person is someone He wants you to be with, right now, and to keep going forward with him. There is a lot of peace that can come from Eucharistic adoration, and discernment often comes in large waves before Him there. While you should also do private discernment before the Blessed Sacrament as you are trying to discern the vocation of marriage, bringing the person who might be the focus of that vocation directly before the Lord at His tabernacle can only be all the more effective.

The Lord blesses those who remember and adore Him in the Blessed Sacrament. Can't the two of you sit with Him for just one hour? Much revelation about each other, and what He is calling you to do about each other, may well take place there.

You might, as you grow further in your relationship, become regular scheduled adorers together, if you have an organized adoration group in your area. If there is a regular Tuesday Holy Hour, or if you can sign up together to be the adorers from 8:00 to 9:00 every Thursday night at the perpetual adoration chapel, you will learn a great deal about whether your friend has the kind of commitment that is required in a Catholic marriage. If someone hesitates to sign up for a regular adoration stint because a basketball game might sometimes be on then, or she doesn't want to sign up because work is always so unpredictable, that should tell you something about where Christ fits into his or her own life, and where He might be placed in your life together.

You might want to make a commitment to going together to the nine consecutive First Friday Masses in honor of the Sacred Heart of Jesus, as was revealed to St. Margaret Mary. Keeping the First Fridays requires that you adore Jesus in the Blessed Sacrament for at least fifteen minutes. Why not make the First Fridays your special Mass/Holy Hour/date night? What better way to be about the discernment of your own heart's desire than to devote this time together to be with Christ and adore his Most Sacred Eucharistic Heart?

4. Be with children together. The Catechism teaches that children are one of the ends or purposes of Catholic marriage (Catechism, para. 2366). Children are the fruit of marriage. They are the couple's love made manifest, the incarnation of their love. Any Catholic marriage must be open to the blessing of children. If you marry, it should be your sincere desire that God blesses your marriage with children. A large part of your life with your spouse will likely be spent in raising your children together, which will be your greatest joy and your greatest challenge. You might as well start to get a read on whether this person will be a good parent as soon as you can. If someone does not have the makings of a good parent, then your discernment should tell you that this person may not be the Catholic spouse that God has planned for you.

Opportunities to be around children are everywhere. If you are in a church group, suggest that you volunteer for the inner-city kids' basketball outing. Or volunteer to work the "crying room" or nursery together during a Mass. Now *that* might be a baptism of fire, but what better way to find out if a man knows what to do with a crying child—or even several of them?

If you have been dating awhile, and if one of you has family who has children, invite your friend to a family outing where the little ones will be, and get down together and play with them. Offer to take them to the park. The other adults will love you for it, and you will have a great opportunity to see how your friend acts with and manages children.

If you have been dating longer still, do someone a real favor and offer to babysit together. Maybe your sister and her husband need an evening away from their four little darlings. Maybe his best friend and his wife recently had a baby and they just want to sleep, while you two take the baby for a walk in the stroller. If you really want to see someone interact with children, offer to babysit for a weekend for a friend's or relative's kids (with only one of you spending the night, of course). Being together for the better part of 24 hours with a houseful of children in their own environment—now *that* could be a real eye-opener.

You might find out that someone is cross and short-tempered and just not able to get along with children at all. You might find out someone is bossy and authoritative, and does not know how to get a child to cooperate. You might find out that someone comes all unglued and is grossed out by runny noses, drooly pacifiers, and dirty diapers. You need to know these things now, before you invest a lot more time in someone who is not ready to handle the reality of having children.

Since married Catholics are to practice chastity and morality in the sacrament and are never to use artificial birth control, it sometimes happens that a baby comes along sooner rather than later in a Catholic marriage. So don't think that if your friend is not very good with the children that "it's okay, we have lots of time before *we* would have our own kids. He would be able to cope by then, I am sure." The patter of little feet could happen in the first year of your marriage. You have no idea what God has planned for you, so you had better be sure early on whether this man or woman is ready to be a parent.

It is true that dealing with children is a skill, and if someone was an only child, or has not been around kids a lot, or never babysat, they might not be as skilled as they would need to be if they were actually a parent to their own children. And people can develop those skills. But if you are thinking "Is she the one?" you are already close enough to the discernment of that question that you need to know at least where she stands on being a parent, so you know where you are and how you both need to improve and grow. People develop and will grow in this parental role, but you need to know where you are starting from and whether you are comfortable with that starting point. If not, the time to end the relationship is now.

Why? Because those children come along sooner than you might think, and things can happen. You are picking a person who might have to raise your children without you, if something should happen to you. Heaven forbid either of you die early in your marriage, but it could happen. Are you confident that this man or woman will properly raise your children, your precious babies, in your absence? Can you trust him or her to provide for them, feed them, clothe them, love them, and raise them in the Catholic faith? You might not think an afternoon of playing with your college roommate's two toddlers can tell you all that, but it might get you on the path to knowing more about that. And that is what discernment is all about.

What you also might find out is that your friend is wonderful with children, kind, loving, fun, can entertain them, can discipline them fairly and with good direction, and has abundant patience, resourcefulness, and energy. Those are all qualities you want in the mother or father of your children. And to find that in the person you are dating will take you a long way on the path to discerning if they are the person God has sent to serve with you in the vocation of marriage and family.

5. Meet the parents. As soon as you possibly can, introduce your friend to one or both of your parents. Try to get a chance to meet your friend's parents, too, as soon as possible. Too often a couple does not take this step early on, and does not try to meet each other's families until they are already engaged. This is a big mistake. There is much insight and discernment that can come from meeting a person's family, their parents in particular.

First, if you are both Catholic, you might have great examples of strong Catholic marriages in your two sets of parents that can be a great yardstick to measure what is growing between the two of you. If you are lucky enough that your parents are still married and are devoutly living the Catholic faith together in their own vocation of marriage, go home to them as soon as you can, not only to allow them to observe the two of you and give their insights, but for you to observe them in the light of their marriage, and compare you and your love interest to what you see in them.

Both sets of parents have something unique to offer your discernment. Even if your parents are not still married (parted by either divorce or death), your parents have valuable insights into marriage and what is necessary to make a go of marriage in this world, and in the Catholic faith.

This is not a suggestion that you have some big meeting with the parents to discuss marriage. That might come at some point. But just going out to dinner with them, letting them see how the two of you relate to each other, how you treat each other, what each of you talks about, and what your goals and dreams are, can be very enlightening. Your love interest might have to answer a question your dad puts to him directly, whereas he might beat around the bush with you. Her mother might be able to shed some interesting light on why your girlfriend does some things the way she does!

Similarly, under the old saying "The apple does not fall far from the tree," seeing your love interest's parents can tell you a lot about what he or she has been exposed to as the standard for marriage. Does his father treat his mother with love and respect? That is what your boyfriend learned, then. If his father is short, snappish, and rude to his mom, somewhere along the way your boyfriend might have learned that is an acceptable way to talk to one's wife. You need to know that. Or your love interest's parents might have had a marriage that he does not want to emulate (it ended in divorce, or was loveless, or lacking in respect), and so he has swung far the other way. But you want to see this firsthand to see why he is the way he is.

Sometimes one or both sets of parents have died already. If this is the case, perhaps there are older married siblings that might be able to reflect those more mature, familial insights for the two of you. Or if you both live far from your families, a "meet the parents" opportunity will only properly come if and when you do become engaged. Then perhaps you can befriend an older Catholic married couple in your parish that can serve as pseudo-parents for the two of you.

You are looking not only for information about your significant other's past, to see how it informs about the future— a future you are testing to see if you should be a part of— but you are also comparing the two of you to what you hope is a good template for a lasting, strong Catholic marriage.

The road to discernment definitely should include frequent stops at your parents' houses.

6. Have a discussion about the Church's teachings on birth control and abortion. The place where the Church's teaching on morality most acutely intersects with human life is in the context of marriage and family. The Church's clear teachings are that abortion in any circumstance is a mortal sin, and that the use of any kind of artificial contraception is gravely immoral. You need to know as soon as possible whether your friend accepts, lives by, and will live by these teachings and beliefs, and if not, you should conclude that they are not God's chosen person for you.

This is not a suggestion to get into a very intimate discussion early on about your future sex life or reproductive decisions. That is a conversation for more advanced discernment. But what needs to be learned early on is what your friend's true views are on these subjects. There are lots of ways to bring the topics up. Try mentioning an abortion clinic or some pro-life activity that is in the news. "There was a rosary rally at the local abortion clinic on Saturday— did you hear about that? What are your views on abortion?" Then you listen. Lots of people give lip service that they don't believe in abortion, but when you hear what they really have to say, you find that they are not completely pro-life.

If someone does not accept the Church's clear teaching on the sanctity of human life in the unborn, is this someone you would even consider as your spouse? The answer must be no, because God would not select for you someone who does not accept the Church's teaching on the sanctity of human life.

The sanctity of human life is not only about abortion, and is not just an issue for the unmarried that find themselves pregnant out of wedlock. The issue enters into marriage as well. You need to be sure that your spouse would make the right decision if faced with issues of infertility, if you were to learn your baby will be born with a handicap or defect (abortion would still be wrong), or if a life-and-death decision of saving a baby *in utero* versus saving the wife's life had to be made (both lives are sacred and an attempt to save both must be made, for the baby cannot simply be sacrificed to save the mother). Is this a person whose beliefs are such that you would want them making those kinds of moral judgments for you, or with you?

Ostensibly the more problematic and more frequently found issue will be about the Church's teaching on birth control. Without getting really graphic, simply ask, "What do you think about the Church's teaching on artificial birth control?" And again, you then just listen. You might find out they don't agree at all, that they think it's none of the Vatican's business what people do in their bedrooms. You might find out they think only methods that interfere with implantation of the embryo (like an intrauterine device) are wrong because they cause abortions, but they think there is nothing wrong with hormonal contraception like birth control pills—but they can act as abortifacients as well. They may think there is nothing the matter with using barrier methods, like condoms and diaphragms, because there can be no abortion with those—but they interfere with the openness to the gift of life, and certainly are a barrier to the full openness and gift of the spouses, each to the other, and are a degradation of the whole person, including their fertility, such that they really are injurious to the marital bond, and thus are also immoral. Or they may think there is nothing wrong with destroying a perfectly good, functioning body system like one's fertility by having a vasectomy or tubal ligation.

And you need to know all this, because every one of these positions is contrary to the Church's clear teaching, and if someone espouses any of those views, they are not the spouse sent for you from God. He would not send you someone that will disagree with you, challenge you, or ever tempt you to sin in this most sacred and intimate aspect of married life.

You will run into lots of these people, even Catholics, who will say things like, "I personally don't see what's wrong with condoms myself." Or "I think it's okay if you can't afford children at the time to use the Pill." These people are seriously misinformed and misguided on this very important part of the faith, and if you become involved with them in a dating relationship, they could well drag you down.

Many, many people are not informed on what the Church teaches in these areas and why. That topic is too large and important a subject to tackle in a book like this. But suffice to say that if you meet someone along your dating path who is a confirmed Catholic but does not understand the Church's teachings, either instruct them by a brief explanation or refer them to the Catechism and other Catholic writings on the subjects, or tell them they need to talk to a priest. And pray for them, because they do need to be enlightened.

But stop dating them—because unless and until they believe in the teachings, they can only be a friend to you, as it could become too tempting if you keep dating them when they hold views that are contrary to God's moral law, the Church's teachings, and your beliefs.

What you should be listening for and hoping to hear in your discussion is for your friend to say, "I don't believe in any form of artificial birth control, and I believe that natural family planning is the only way for anyone, especially a married Catholic couple." The person who answers like that could well be the person that God has prepared for you.

7. **Attend the sacrament of reconciliation together.** There is no greater gift of the Church than the opportunity

to be reconciled to the Lord in the sacrament of reconciliation. God's mercy waits for us in the confessional, if we will only go to Him and receive His abundant gift of grace. All have sinned and fallen short. We as humans are in a fallen state in this world, and each of us sins every day, in large and small ways. If you are both Catholics, you should be receiving this sacrament regularly anyway. Why not suggest you go together?

Of course, this is not a suggestion to actually *confess* together, but to go to church for the sacrament together. You meet at church together, and bring along an examination of conscience (widely available at churches, in Catholic bookstores, and in prayer books). Sit and read it silently together. Sit there together as each of you goes over each commandment in your own mind—what you have done in violation of that commandment, how you have fallen short. Sit there for a while, not speaking but being together in your own brokenness, reflecting on your own sinfulness. And use that time also to see how your friend responds to the experience. Are there tears or other indications of a contrite heart? Looking at one's own sinfulness should be a deeply moving experience. If someone is not somber and contrite in the midst of examining their conscience before God, that is something you need to notice.

Then you each take your turn with the priest in the reconciliation room or confessional, as the case may be, and receive the sacrament of reconciliation. After you each have received the sacrament and have taken time in the church to do your penance privately (if it is the kind of penance, like prayers, that can be done right then, as opposed to some other act Father gives to you to do), come back together, leave the church, and talk about the experience.

What does he think about God's mercy? What does it mean to him? How does she feel after receiving the sacrament? There should be a lot of gratitude and peacefulness in your friend right now, and you can be there to see that, to see the signs that they are really living their faith, and are changed by the mercy that God has shown to them.

Having the experience of going to the sacrament together might lead to conversations between you that can be very revealing and therefore helpful to your discernment. For example, if you know you're going to go to confession together every two weeks, you might be more likely to talk about sin as it affects your own relationship. Sometimes couples get into real trouble and sin with their physical/sexual relationship. It is a great temptation when you are attracted to someone you think you might want to marry. Most of us would not consider being sexual or unchaste with just any random person off the street. We're Catholic, we think; we have "morals," right? But the excuse that "we did it because we are in love; that makes it all right, doesn't it, and we are probably getting married someday anyway" is *not* God's standard, and it's still a sin if you are unmarried, even if you love each other.

But if you know that you are going to have to examine your conscience alongside the person who is in the unique position to know if you have been involved in any sexual sin, and that you are going to hold each other accountable before the Lord twice a month in confession about your relationship, you can be assured that the two of you will be well on your way to living the kind of holy and chaste premarital relationship that is the necessary foundation for the chastity that will be required in your marital relationship, if that is where God is calling you.

You might learn a lot from this process. It might lead to conversation that reveals what your partner's "unsurrendered areas" might be. What does that mean? Many faithful people are quick to accept that Jesus is their Savior and that He died for their sins. But Jesus is also Lord, and that means he has to be Lord over all your life—all areas of it. Most people are able to give over a lot of themselves and their lives to the Lordship of Jesus, but most people hold back something, some sin area which they reserve for themselves still, where they still want to be "lord" themselves. That is an "unsurrendered area" that they don't want to make Jesus the Lord over yet. It is often sex or unchastity, or intemperance, like drinking or overeating, or it might be work and money. Your unsurrendered areas are identifiable by those sins you find yourself confessing over and over again.

It's helpful to find out about your partner's unsurrendered areas, and going to confession together might reveal that. You do that by seeing where they feel they are falling short and sinning over and over. Now, you might know that your boyfriend has trouble controlling his drinking. But does he see it as a problem, an unsurrendered area, that he confesses? That is information you might find helpful in your discernment. It might also show you ways that you can be a good helpmate to him that you might not have thought of before (like not having beer in your house, or suggesting dates somewhere other than bars or clubs).

Going to confession alone is hard enough for many Catholics, but don't hesitate any longer. There is strength in numbers, so go together. And don't hesitate to see if your love interest is someone who is eager to drink from the fountain of God's mercy in the sacrament of reconciliation. You won't be sorry you tried it.

8. Get spiritual direction together from a priest. As your relationship continues, and you are getting into a more serious discernment, it can be very beneficial to talk to a priest together, even before you are engaged. That is usually the only time when most couples seek out a priest, in order to reserve the church for the wedding and get signed up for the Pre-Cana or Engaged Encounter programs the parish offers to those preparing for marriage. But really, the priests are there too for the couple who is still "just dating." Talking to a priest together can do a great deal of good on your path to discernment.

First, this is not something you do in early casual dating. To do this, you really need to have a committed relationship. But if you are exclusively dating, and are serious, why not suggest that the two of you talk to Father?

Maybe you invite your parish priest out to dinner, or over to one of your homes for dinner. This will first give the priest a chance to see the two of you interact and get to know you better as individuals and as a couple. Take this social opportunity to ask Father if he would meet with the two of you together for the purpose of some spiritual direction about your relationship, and how God might be calling you together. Most priests would be thrilled to hear this from any couple. There are so many bad marriages, divorces, requests for annulments, and so many broken hearts in the Church today that could have been spared if those couples had just done what is being suggested here.

When you meet with the priest for direction, let him lead you both with his questions and suggestions. It will be informative to see how your partner interacts with Father and how he takes his comments, direction, and suggestions. Part of our Catholic faith is obedience and submission to the authority of the Church. The priest at the local level represents that authority. Seeing how your partner takes to that direction, whether he is respectful of it, is very important. Father might also have some words of caution for you, or some observations you might not want to hear. But hearing them together is an important step on your discernment journey.

This could also be a time of learning for one or both of you. Perhaps some of the other techniques you've tried from this list have led you to have questions about, say, contraception, chastity, or something else about the Catholic faith and teaching. This time spent together with a priest when you can ask questions and get the *right* answers, and hear them together at the same time, will help you both be very clear about these matters which you need to know and understand.

9. Attend a retreat together. On the path to more serious discernment, the process of seeking out the answer of whether a particular person is God's chosen spouse for you needs your focus and attention. It is very hard to find the quiet time to reflect and pray on what should be the most important decision of your life: the choice of a husband or a wife. So shouldn't you set aside some time where you both can do that? Going on a spiritual retreat would be an excellent way to bring this kind of opportunity into your lives. After you have been dating awhile and trying to figure out how God is calling you, why not seek out a spiritual retreat together?

Choose a retreat that is for both sexes, and that is at least 24 hours long. You need at least that much time to decompress and put off all your cares of the world, and really focus in your heart on the stirrings of the Spirit on this important issue.

It should be a retreat that affords you lots of time for silent prayer, spiritual reading, contemplation, meditation, Mass, Eucharistic adoration, and quiet time to be alone and together. Before you leave for the retreat, each of you might give the other a list of questions or issues you are concerned about or questioning that you want the other to pray on in particular during the retreat. God might answer some of your prayer questions through your partner instead of directly to you.

If your partner is willing to go on a retreat with you, this shows that he or she really wants to make the pursuit of faith with you a priority, to take a whole weekend out for God, for prayer, for contemplation, and to do it with you. That should speak volumes.

And don't be surprised if over the course of the retreat many good insights come to you and your partner about what God is calling you each to do. God loves it when we give Him our focused attention. What better way to do that than on a retreat?

10. "Fast" from each other with a separation. After some period of dating has taken place, if you are trying to discern the stirrings of your heart about your partner, the surefire, fastest way to see if he or she might be the person God has sent to you is to *not see the person.* That is right: stop dating. "Fast" from him or her in order to see what it is you really feel about the person.

The concept of fasting from anything has become foreign to most of us. To do without something we want in our culture is almost unheard of. But the spiritual merits of fasting, be that fasting from food, or television, or some habit, or something we enjoy, even from the person we care about, can be a very effective way to find out what is really in your heart, and what is in their heart as well.

Let's be totally clear: this is not a suggestion that you "break up." Rather, it is taking a little time apart to get some perspective. It is not that you want to end the relationship, but you want to test what is really going on by trying to be apart for a short time. If you are the person suggesting the fast, make sure your partner understands this well, so no false conclusions are made that you're really just trying to dump your partner.

Maybe you impose on yourselves that you are not going to see or talk to each other for one week. Such a fast has to be by an act of your wills. Don't just use some previously planned vacation one of you has set as the time of being apart. No, this suggestion is that, in the midst of your normal daily lives, you *choose* to give each other up for a week— even though you could see and talk to each other, and want to see and talk to each other, you impose on yourselves this "fasting" from each other to see how it makes each of you feel, and see what it reveals to each of you.

There is a well-known wealthy business tycoon who does something he calls "random acts of deprivation." Even though he surely does not have to do without anything in this world, given his vast wealth, he occasionally deprives himself of something, just to see what it is like and to see what he learns from the deprivation. For example, instead of being chauffeured to his office, he took public transportation to work for a week and found out that his city needed some serious transit improvements if his employees were going to be able to get to work easily. Or, instead of fancy meals, he will bring his lunch in a paper sack for a week. Or maybe he will even fly coach. He gets all kinds of insights from such deprivations.

This suggests that you engage in a "random act of deprivation" from each other by this fast, just to see what you learn about yourself and your partner from the experience.

You might find out that you miss him or her terribly, and even feel that you can't stand being without him, or not talking to her. That is a pretty important thing to find out, and you would not know that if you didn't, by an act of your will, deny your being together.

There is a great saying by a French duke, François, duc de La Rochefoucauld: "Absence diminishes mediocre passions, and increases great ones, as the wind blows out candles and fans fires." Being apart from your love for a time can often tell more about what you feel than a much longer time spent together. You might find that your feelings are much deeper than you ever knew, or even that you are completely in love with the person. That would be a good sign, and something you need to know.

Or maybe something else quite different will happen during the fast. You might find that you are really appreciating the solitude, that being on your own feels good to you somehow, and that while you care about your friend, your life does not feel that different with or without him in it on a daily basis. That is also something you might not know if you didn't "fast" from him for a while.

Make sure that you both do your best not to "break the fast"—don't cheat and sneak in a phone call or send an e-mail. Take this fast seriously and more discernment will come from it than if you cheat and break the fast. It's like dieting—it works better if you don't cheat.

Here is what not to do, however. Don't date other people while you are on your fast. This is not about looking for someone else while you are apart. If you go on dates with others during the fast, that will just fill some of the void left by the person you are fasting from and won't give you a clear picture of what you are feeling for that person.

Also, don't make the fast open-ended in time. Pick a certain period of time and plan from the start what your next time together is going to be. For example, "We are not going to talk or e-mail or see each other for the next two weeks, but two weeks from this Saturday, we are going out at 7 p.m. for dinner at our favorite restaurant and then for a long walk so we can talk about what we learned during our fast." This will give each of you the assurance that this is not just some chickenhearted way of trying to break up with each other but really is about discerning what you each see about yourselves, each other, and the relationship.

To do this takes courage, but so does marriage. It's not for the faint of heart, and you need to have these experiences to prepare yourself for that.

After your relationship has become serious, and you are close to entering into the final phase of discernment as to whether you are called together to the sacrament of marriage, seriously consider a more substantial fast, a desert experience, of going your separate ways for a time to really confirm to yourself, and in turn be able to confirm to your partner, whether you feel called to the vocation of marriage together.

A forty-day fast from each other, actually being "broken up" from each other, during which time each is free to do whatever they want, including date others if they care to, allows you to really test if the person you have been with *really* is who you want to be with. This is a very powerful tool of discernment for the vocation of marriage.

Jesus went into the desert for forty days and nights and fasted before he began the most important work of His life, His public ministry. If you think you are being called to your life's most important work—that is, marriage with a particular person—should you not at least do the same?

Each of you needs to be on your own, without the influence of the other, to discern alone about what is right for you as an individual, as opposed to you together as a couple. There could be secret doubts that you have that need a chance to come up to the surface and be examined, and that might never happen if you are seeing her smile every day, the light of which has a way of covering over doubts. There could be deep questions that you need to ask, but you don't even know the questions yet because the two of you are so busy running around together, dating, serving in the Church, and having all the fun that couples have. You need to step back from this and go into the desert to hear the questions, and the answers, of your own heart.

This longer fast in the context of a more serious relationship definitely has to have a specified closing date to it, and the forty-day period is a good amount of time. It allows for four or five weekends without each other that can serve as opportunities for each of you to try socializing with others, even have dates with someone else.

That is important—to actually give each other permission to have dates with other people. If you have been going out exclusively for a while, you may have forgotten what it's like, and since in marriage you are "forsaking all others," it's better to know now that your boyfriend is really not done with his partying days and wants to be free to go out and see other women.

If you have been focusing on one man, you might have forgotten that there are a lot of fish in the sea, and that men find you attractive and will ask you out when you are unattached and not seen as part of a couple. And maybe you are not ready to give that up yet. You won't know that unless you are "fasting."

Another thing that might be very helpful while you are fasting "in the desert" is to each keep a journal or write letters to each other that you will save up and share with the other at the end of your fast. Forty days is a long time, and there might be insights that you have early on in the process that you want to make sure you remember so you can share them later with your partner.

This longer fast must have a scheduled anticipated reunion at its conclusion. You both need to know that you are going to spend a whole day and evening together once it is over, catching up on all that has happened in your lives during the fast, and sharing all that you have come to realize while you were apart.

It would not be surprising if some proposals of marriage come on that 41st day, or that some really profound answers have been placed in both of your hearts. It might be that you are called together to marriage, or maybe not, or maybe not yet. But whatever the conclusion, that forty days apart probably will reveal more to you than months or even years of dating might. Better to know either way now, because life is so precious and short that you need to either move forward together or get on with your life and find that person that God really does have planned for you.

So don't be afraid to fast from each other. Fasting from one another, when it's offered as a sacrifice and with a seeking heart, will bring forth answers and graces faster than anything else. And that is what you want. You want to discern as soon as you can, as well as you can.

A time of fasting or "continence" apart is also a good

lesson that can be applied to the sacrifice and the chastity that are required in marriage. If you get married, there will be times when the two of you will have to be apart for an extended period, like during military service, or the illness of a family member, or travel for work. You need to know that you can get along without each other if you have to. You might not otherwise know this. If your girlfriend falls apart during the forty days and is a total mess without you around, that tells you something about the strengths and weaknesses of the woman you are wondering may be your wife. If your boyfriend's apartment devolves into something like a college frat house when he is living without daily visits from you, who are always doing his dishes and picking up his magazines, that tells you something, too.

There is also a symbolic aspect of this time of continence, and that is there will be times in marriage when you can't have sexual intercourse, either because you are practicing natural family planning, and it is the wife's fertile phase and you are abstaining from sexual activity, or during the final weeks of pregnancy, or in the weeks after the birth of a baby, or a miscarriage, or even just during times of great activity, work demands, or other stress or distractions in life. You need to know that your partner can get along without something. Getting along without sex is just one such thing. To test how they get along without you completely for a time can only tell you more and reveal more to you about this aspect of the person. Is he or she someone who can abstain, get along without? Because there are these kinds of things in marriage that are going to come along. Better to see it now and test it now, than regret later.

I can hear the cries and protests now: "But what if he decides he really wants someone else and not me while we are apart?" You already know the answer to that: it means that he is not the man that God has selected to be *your* husband. "What if she decides that what she really wants is to go to med school instead of following me in my career?"

Then it means that she is probably not the woman God wants for you to marry (at least not at this point).

Don't fear the truth that comes from this fast and learning what is in your partner's heart. You do not want to marry anyone who is not as completely in love with you as you are with them, or someone who doesn't want exactly the same things from the relationship and from a life together that you do. I promise you, you *don't* want it. And if you delude yourself now into thinking you do, you will likely pay for it later in the form of a bad relationship, a broken marriage, divorce, broken hearts, and hurt, innocent children. You don't want any of that, and a fast now might well save you from all of that.

If the forty-day fast leads one of you to conclude that you are not called to marriage together, or are not called at the moment, then so be it. You should engage in the communal discernment suggested in Chapter 12 to make sure you have discerned as best you can. But if there is certitude about your conclusion, know that even if it is not God's absolute will (assuming that He does intend for you to be together), it is at least His permissive will—He allows it to be so—that one of you has reached this conclusion. He is allowing your partner to have doubts, be on a different schedule, have a different life agenda, and most importantly, exercise his or her free will, the most important gift of personhood God has placed in each of us. Don't interfere with that. Your partner has a free will that is God-given, and it is his or her right to exercise that free will. So let your partner reach his or her own conclusion.

Remember, what you want is God's right spouse for you. That is what you want, and don't settle for anything less. And don't try to contrive something different out of your partner if that is not what you both want. It will get you nowhere. A fast will help you in all these ways.

Conclusion. These are ten catalysts, ten "speed dating" techniques, to try to distill more quickly what God's will is concerning someone you are dating. Some are meant for earlier in the relationship, others are meant for later. But each one represents a very good way to find out the kind of things you need to know, about matters of faith and belief, about the feelings of your own heart and those of your partner. All of it can only be of help to you in making the discernment of whether the person you are dating might be God's chosen husband or wife for you.

It also should be said that if you as a couple have not done all or most of these ten things, you probably have not done enough to discern if you are called to the vocation of marriage together. If you have not prayed together, gone to church for the sacraments and Mass, met family, discussed basic things about the faith, and tested your feelings by being apart, then you have not done the necessary evidence-gathering that is needed for true discernment of this important decision. If you think that you can just wait and find out later, when you are engaged or, worse yet, after you are married, you are sorely mistaken.

Similarly, if you are dating someone who is Catholic and who otherwise seems like a good person for you, but you are just not "bowled over" by the person yet, you should still be trying all these things—because, until you have seen this person in the circumstances suggested by this list, you might be denying yourself the opportunity that God has selected for when He is going to reveal to you the "exclamation" He has planned for you about that person. For example, maybe it will be in a moment when she is holding your sister's baby that you might look at this woman that before you saw as just some girl you were dating at the moment, and you see her for the first time as a mother of a child, maybe your child together. You might start to recognize things in her that you didn't see before, and you start to get "bowled over." That's the exclamation. Until you have tried and tested a person in these kinds of situations, if they are otherwise a good Catholic and a good match for you in general, you really need to keep discerning. Because God just might not have taken you to that point of the "exclamation" yet.

So use these techniques, these catalysts, whether you already feel your heart falling for the person or even if you don't really feel in love yet. Either way, they will surely help you in your discernment.

Chapter 7

They Recognized Him in the Breaking of the Bread

The biggest trouble you might have could be in recognizing the person that God has sent to you. You might think that it would be easy, that you will just know right away, but that is not how it usually happens. Some people think they know they have found "the one" the moment they lay eyes on the person (Adam in the garden seemed to know right away that Eve was the one for him). Others feel they know fairly early on. For still others, it took quite some time for them to "recognize" the person as the man or woman of their dreams and prayers. What accounts for the difference? How and when and where will you know? If you don't feel something right away, does that mean this person is not "the one" for you?

There might be some clues in holy Scripture. Let's look at the Gospel of Luke, after the Resurrection, when Jesus appeared to the disciples. We can't forget that the disciples had been with Jesus in His lifetime, lived with Him day in and day out, and heard Him speak and teach firsthand. You would certainly think that they would have been able to recognize Him when they saw Him, when He talked to them. Surely they would have had in mind His prediction to them that He would die a horrible death and then rise again from the dead; you would think that would have stuck with them and they would have been expecting Him, hopeful that they would see Him again. But after He died, their mindset was apparently such that their eyes were closed to "see" Him, to recognize Him, if they encountered Him. When Jesus first appeared to the two disciples on the road to Emmaus, they didn't recognize Him from what He said to them. Even on the road with Him for hours, from His teaching and conversation and appearance, His own disciples didn't recognize Him. As the Scripture verse continues, we see what happened next:

> So they drew near to the village to which they were going. He appeared to be going further, but they constrained him, saying, "Stay with us, for it is toward evening and the day is now far spent." So he went in to stay with them. When he was at table with them, he took the bread and blessed, and broke it, and gave it to them. And their eyes were opened and *they recognized him*; and he vanished out of their sight. (Luke 24:28-31, emphasis added)

The two disciples then recounted to the other disciples what had taken place on the way to Emmaus, and "how he was known to them in the breaking of the bread" (Luke 24:35).

The disciples had no idea who Jesus was until they recognized Him, until they knew it was Him, "in the breaking of the bread." Even Jesus was not known to those who knew Him best until He did this act in their presence, the thing that reflected most fully who He was. He gave His flesh for the life of the world. The Eucharistic sacrifice, which is the breaking of the bread—the offering of His Body for all of us, for our sins—was the heart and soul of Jesus' mission, the thing that He was sent to earth to do. So that is where He was most Himself, most who He was, the manner in which He would be most readily identified. Yes, He was a teacher, a rabbi, and He taught them on the road, and the two disciples were impressed by what they heard, but they didn't recognize Him from His words and insights alone on the road. While they didn't know who He was, they knew somehow they didn't want to part company with this Stranger, and invited Him to stay with them longer. But it was not until He broke the bread that they "saw" He was the Lord. They knew Him, they recognized Him, only in the breaking of the bread, and then everything that went before made sense.

There is something to be learned from that. Recognition of who someone is to be to you might not come right away. The two disciples spent a whole day's walk with Jesus but didn't understand that it was Him until they saw Him that evening "in the breaking of the bread." It might be that you need to see someone when they are in a situation in which they are most who they really are—that activity or place or task or setting where God most wants them to be, where their key mission is, where they are most fully themselves— for you to recognize them as the person that God has sent to you.

It might be the first time you see the woman you are dating interact with a child. Maybe the greatest thing she is called to be is a mother, that is, the mother to your children in particular, but you won't recognize her, your eyes won't be opened to her, until you have a chance to see her hold and cuddle a little child. And when you see that, you really "see" her for the first time as the woman God has sent to you.

Maybe you won't recognize a man as your husband un- til you see him about his work, doing what is his passion, his life's mission, how skilled he is at it, how capable, and how he has the respect of his colleagues. Maybe then you will see him as the man God has sent to you, for you to respect, to submit yourself to, and for him to provide for you and keep you safe.

The lesson of this Scripture is to not dismiss someone too soon, before you have had enough time together to make sure you have seen the person in enough of the right circumstances to "recognize" them. If the two disciples had just said "See ya" to Jesus when they reached the village, gone their separate ways, and not invited Jesus to stay with them longer, they never would have understood who it was who had been with them and taught them on the road. If they had cut Him off too soon and never been at table with Him, they never would have had the chance to recognize Him "in the breaking of the bread."

The moral of the story is that if there is a person in your life who is a devout Catholic, who meets all the criteria for someone that could be your holy spouse, you have things in common with that person, and you like them and are attracted to them, but you just haven't felt "the exclamation" for them yet, don't give up on them. If there is every reason that the two of you should be a match in God's eyes but you just don't quite see it yet, it's terribly important that you keep trying to be with the person in situations where they are most authentically themselves.

Ask them to suggest dates or outings for the two of you. Tell them you want to do the things they would enjoy. Tell them you want to tag along on some of their family outings or go along with them to their charity or volunteer activities. Do all you can to be with the person in their most natural settings, where you can see them as they really are, in those places and activities where they have their joy, where it seems God has really placed them, where it seems God is using them most.

It is in seeing this person in these settings where he or she is most authentically going about the reason they are here (as Jesus' reason for being was to be our Paschal Lamb and give Himself, His Body, as a sacrifice for us), the more likely it is that you might recognize him or her in what is "the breaking of the bread" for them. Your eyes might be opened and, like the disciples, you will be glad you didn't just say "See ya later" and go on your merry way.

Think of what a tragedy it would be if you get to heaven someday and the Lord tells you that your chosen spouse was someone that you gave up on. How awful will that be— to learn that you defeated the will of God and passed up having a holy sacramental marriage, a wonderful spouse, and perhaps the blessings of children and a family, and the generation upon generation through the ages that would have come after you, just because you gave up on the person before you happened to have a chance to see them, to recognize them, in the "breaking of the bread" that was to be the circumstance or sign of recognition for you?

While at some point you may be able to feel you have enough indication that a person is *not* the one that God has sent to you—and exactly what point that is, only you can say—but unless there is a pressing reason to move on, don't give up too soon, because recognition might still be forthcoming, and you will be glad you hung in there.

Chapter 8

Catherine of Alexandria Syndrome

If you are a devout Catholic who longs for marriage and has lived your life in a manner worthy of the high calling to that sacrament, it might surprise you to find out that somewhere along the way you may have contracted "Catherine of Alexandria syndrome."

Yikes, you say, is that serious? Well, yes, it can be a very serious condition if not diagnosed and treated. It's an ophthalmologic condition that affects your vision. If left unchecked, it can jeopardize the happy and holy life you are seeking with a spouse in marriage. Before you become alarmed, be assured there is a treatment, but you have to start by understanding the etiology of the condition and its symptoms.

First, who was Catherine of Alexandria, anyway? She was a virgin and martyr of the early Christian Church. She is still highly venerated in the Eastern church. She was a saint, but the Roman Catholic Church no long celebrates her feast day, probably because her legend was not verifiable to its strict standards of confirmation. But her life still has an important message for Catholic singles today who seek the vocation of marriage.

Catherine lived in the city of Alexandria, Egypt, during the reigns of the pagan Roman emperors Maximian, Maxentius, and Maximinus (A.D. 305-313). She was the daughter of Konstas (or Costis), the ruler of Alexandria.

She was patrician, of noble birth, and very wealthy. She was born a pagan in the Roman Empire at the time when Christianity was on the rise, and with it, the persecution of Christians.

Catherine was by all accounts extraordinary—tall, incomparably beautiful, graceful, and filled with such generosity, charm, and virtue that she was adored by all. She was also extremely intelligent and gifted in many disciplines, including philosophy and medicine. She studied and had complete command of the writings of Plato and Socrates. She had a great gift for speaking many languages and was an eloquent orator. And she was a chaste virgin, which, even in her pagan culture, was a highly esteemed trait.

Having so many gifts, talents, and virtues, Catherine was a very sought-after young woman. Today we might call her a "real catch." Princes, noblemen, and senators all wanted her hand in marriage.

Legend is a bit unclear on this, but apparently Catherine's father died when she was only fourteen years old, and then she herself became the ruler of Alexandria. Her mother, Sabinella, was frequently approached by wealthy and highly esteemed men who sought Catherine as a bride. Many men wanted to possess Catherine, not only for her great beauty and virtue, but also for political reasons. Her mother counseled Catherine to hurry up and marry so that her father's estate would not be jeopardized. After much argument, Catherine agreed to marry, but she had one condition.

Catherine's condition was this: since she herself was so beautiful, so rich, so noble, so virtuous, so smart, and so pure, she would accept a man as her husband only if he were just like her in every attribute: as smart as she was clever, as handsome as she was beautiful, as pure as she was virginal, as studious as she was learned, as well-spoken as she was articulate, and so on down the list.

So Sabinella and her noble family tried to find such a man for Catherine. They really tried. They presented suitor after suitor to Catherine, but Catherine found some fault with each one of them. She refused any suitor who was unacceptable or unworthy of or inferior to her in any way.

Legend has it that Catherine's mother was a Christian, but a secret believer, for fear of persecution. And Catherine's mother soon realized that it was absolutely impossible to find a man perfect enough to be a husband to Catherine. After many tries to persuade Catherine of any man's worthiness, Catherine's mother sought out her own secret spiritual confessor for advice. He was a hermit and ascetic who lived in hiding outside Alexandria.

Sabinella took Catherine to visit the hermit. He, too, could see Catherine's many great virtues. Then he told Catherine about Christ, about how wonderful and virtuous He was. But apparently he didn't make clear that he was talking about a heavenly King. Catherine thought he was describing some human prince, and was very interested and eager to meet such a man, thinking she was finally hearing of someone who was worthy of her for marriage. Begging that she might see such a virtuous man, the hermit gave Catherine an icon of the Blessed Virgin with the Christ child and told her to go home and pray before it.

Catherine did just that, and had a mystical dream of the Virgin Mary presenting her to this perfect Christ, who, quite surprisingly, would not accept her, who actually turned His back on her and would not even receive her. Catherine was very confused and upset about this, for she took this to mean that she was not worthy of Him, which was a first for her— a rude awakening, you might say.

Distraught, Catherine returned to the hermit and told him about the dream, desperate to find a way to make this Perfect Man love her. So he instructed Catherine in the Christian faith. Because Catherine was so smart, she was able to understand in just one session, and was baptized a Christian.

Thereafter, following the hermit's direction, Catherine prayed and fasted, and asked the Virgin to appear to her again. Catherine then had another dream in which the Blessed Mother again presented her to Christ, who this time received her with great love, as she now in truth possessed all the virtues and graces that really mattered in Christ's eyes. Then Christ gave Catherine a ring and betrothed her to Himself as His mystical virgin bride. When Catherine awoke from her dream, there was a real golden ring on her finger. This betrothal of Catherine to Christ has been depicted in many great works of art through the centuries.

In case you are wondering about the rest of Catherine's story, she went on to be martyred for her faith by the Emperor Maximinus. He tried to torture Catherine on the wheel, which collapsed when she was placed on it. Maximinus ordered her imprisoned and starved, but it is said that while in jail angels ministered to her, and a dove brought her food. Catherine was eventually beheaded because that was apparently the only method that could bring about her death. Catherine died a virgin martyr for the Faith around A.D. 310.

So what can we learn from Catherine? And just what is her "syndrome"?

It is that maybe, just maybe, we are being too picky. Like Catherine, we each need to prayerfully and humbly look at ourselves and see if we are seeking only that person who is an absolute exact match to us or, even worse, someone who is so virtuous that only Christ Himself could possibly ever meet the description of the person we want for a spouse.

It's easy to develop this "syndrome." It sneaks up on you, in a way. When you have been a "good Catholic" all your life, have preserved yourself for your spouse in sexual purity, have been a "good girl" or "good boy" and done everything right, have been a good daughter or son, sister or brother, friend, student, worker, have taken good care of yourself, kept yourself up, dieted, worked out, worn nice clothes, worked hard to get a good education, succeeded in a good job, saved your money, supported yourself, been kind and charitable and helpful to others, and have not messed up in any appreciable way, it's easy to slip into Catherine's way of thinking: that any person who is good enough for me has to match me in all my virtues. So what's wrong with that?

The problem is that it can be very dangerous, and keep us from the fulfillment of our vocation to marriage. If a person is not as cute as we are cute, we reject them as "not attractive enough." Or if the person doesn't live in our part of the country, we reject them as a country bumpkin, or a "Yankee," or declare them otherwise "geographically unacceptable." Or, if a person does not have the education we do, they are "not smart enough" for us.

Or maybe the person has a job we consider dull and boring—then they are "not ambitious enough" for us. Or maybe their job is their passion, but is not all that lucrative, so they are "not financially stable enough" for us.

Or maybe it's that the person has not been as pure as we have been; maybe their sexual history is not as chaste as our own. (It's especially hard for the guys to run that gauntlet successfully.) We think, what, I saved myself for someone who has slept around a lot? No way, we say.

Or maybe the person has not been as faithful to the Church all their life as we have. Perhaps the person was a lapsed Catholic for a while, and is now a "revert" to the faith. Or maybe they are not quite as devout as we are now—they don't go to daily Mass or confession as often as we do, or say the rosary every day. And we decide that is not good enough for us either, in our "holier than thou" way of thinking.

Or maybe the person has made a mistake in judgment somewhere along the way—had a bad first marriage or a child out of wedlock. And we decide that what Christ Himself has redeemed is still not redeemed enough for a Catholic of our high virtues.

Not only can you easily slip into this "matchy-matchy" kind of mind-set—that if someone is not just like you, forget it—an even more serious complication of the "syndrome" is to expect the perfection of Christ in a mere mortal human being, as the hermit faked out Catherine into thinking such a perfect man for her actually existed.

There is indeed Someone so virtuous, so pure, so holy, so wonderful, so gifted as Catherine longed for, that we all long for, but none of us are worthy of Him, unless and until we put on the humility of His salvation and redemption and see that in comparison to Him, we are all most unworthy of His love. Only then do we become everything beautiful and desired and highly esteemed in His eyes.

The truth is this: the only perfect person that ever walked the earth did so 2,000 years ago, and now reigns in glory in heaven at the Father's right hand. Every other man and woman (and that includes the ones who live here on earth for us to know and love and select a spouse from) will have all messed up somehow or other, or be imperfect in some way. So if you are looking for someone who is the perfect combination of Einstein, Brad Pitt, Prince William, Bill Gates, and Jesus Christ, or Julia Roberts, Princess Grace, and the Virgin Mary, all rolled into one mortal man or woman, be assured, you are never going to find such a perfect person.

Perfection is found in Christ alone.

Does that mean, then, that we are all destined to be mystical virgin spouses of Christ, since He alone is perfect enough for the likes of such prizes as ourselves? Not necessarily. Most all of us are called to the vocation of marriage with a "mere" mortal human man or woman; you wouldn't be reading this book if you didn't believe that in your heart.

So how is it, you ask, that I know so much about "Catherine of Alexandria syndrome"? Well, you see, I was diagnosed myself, and I'll tell you, while the diagnosis is somewhat scary, there is a treatment for it that is very simple and very effective. You need a prescription for a special pair of eyeglasses. They are "Christ-colored glasses," and they correct the problem right away.

Looking through these Christ-colored glasses—that is, through the redemptive and loving eyes of Christ—you see every person you meet, date, and court, not in comparison to your own list of virtues but as Christ sees them, now, in this moment, at this point in their faith walk and their life path. (God is not done with any of us yet, you know.) The glasses allow you to look at every person you encounter and see him or her through Christ's eyes. They allow you to see what the Lord sees in a person, as they are today, redeemed from the past, and hopeful in Christ's mercy for the future. You will find out that how the Lord sees a person is probably not how you would have seen that person, looking through all your filters and tests and requirements. And you can bet that the Lord sees that person in the same way He saw Catherine after her conversion—as possessing the qualities and virtues that *really* matter to Him, and which should be the qualities that matter most to us, too, as seeking and holy people of God.

The kicker is that Catherine possessed all her high ideals when she was a pagan herself. When she presented herself to Christ, with all the virtues the world esteemed in her (beauty, wit, brains, high birth), Christ was not impressed. That is not what He is looking for in us. Once she humbled herself to receive the Good News and be baptized, she became the true beautiful and virtuous woman that was foreshadowed by her worldly attributes.

The real human beings we meet in our lives, and we ourselves, are that way too. What the world esteems, and what we might have been lulled into believing we should esteem in a spouse, might have become a little warped and out of whack along the way. It happens.

So I invite you to get tested for "Catherine of Alexandria syndrome." And if you find out you have even a slight case of it, I highly recommend you try some Christ-colored glasses. By looking at every person you date with Christ's vision, and not through your own (maybe, just maybe) slightly perfectionistic scope, you never know what, or whom, you might find—maybe even the fulfillment of your vocation to marriage with a spouse who (as Christ sees it) matches you perfectly.

Chapter 9

The Discernment of Sexual Attraction

You skipped ahead to this chapter, didn't you? The title of this chapter alone seems like an oxymoron—that you could go through a holy process like "discernment" on a topic like sexual attraction. But sex is a very holy topic, and your sexual attraction to the person you are discerning about for the vocation of marriage is a very holy pursuit, and not an oxymoron at all.

We saw from the creation account in Genesis that Adam recognized Eve, he found his exclamation for her, at least in part, in her sexuality. He related to her as a female person in relation to himself as a male person. He connected to her in the Garden of Eden and knew she was the partner suitable for him, at least in part from her sexuality. For us too, sexual attraction should be a part of the information-gathering process in the discernment of Catholic marriage.

Contrary to secular and popular belief, the Church is not "down" on sex at all. In fact, the Church is very much "up" on sex—sex as God intended it to be. Your sexuality is one of the greatest gifts God has given to you. Your body is a temple of the Holy Spirit. God has raised the union between husband and wife to the level of a sacrament of the Church. The "marital embrace" (the beautiful term that the Church often uses to describe sexual intercourse) is an important aspect of the sacrament of marriage.

Here is a beautiful image to ponder: when a married

couple makes love, four angels come and stand post at the corners of their bed, because God is truly present in their sexual union. When the married couple makes love, the Holy Spirit, the Lord and Giver of Life, is there with them, ready to create life with them and through them in their loving marital embrace. This image is awe-inspiring. There is a holiness in sex when it is lived in the context God intended, which means within the context of sacramental marriage.

If you have not done so, run, don't walk, to your nearest Catholic bookstore and buy, read, study, and know well two outstanding works by the Holy Father, Pope John Paul II: *Love and Responsibility* and *The Theology of the Body*. The Holy Father wrote *Love and Responsibility* in 1960, long before he was elected pope. It is a beautiful exegesis of the sanctity of human sexuality and the holy expression of God's amazing gift in the context of Christian marriage.

The Theology of the Body is a collection of the Holy Father's Wednesday audience sermons given each week in Rome to the pilgrims during the first five years of his pontificate, from 1979 to 1984. Each week he talked on the deep spiritual meaning of human sexuality and marital love. Addressing this most important topic of the human experience was the first thing the Holy Father wanted to preach about to the faithful, over the course of 129 sermons. And who says the Church is down on sex?

John Paul II's gift for understanding and explaining the transcendence of the human condition may well someday be his greatest legacy as the successor of Peter, his greatest gift to the Church. While some of his deeply intellectual writing can be tough going in parts, keep with it. You will not be sorry you put in the effort.

If you need some help with *Love and Responsibility*, there is a wonderful Web site at www.catholicculture.com that contains a series of book club-like meeting summaries from young people who have read and studied the Holy Father's book. It is a valuable tool for understanding this great work.

There is also the book *Love and Responsibility: A Simplified Version*, by Monsignor Vincent Walsh, which is a synopsis of each section of the Holy Father's work. It's a good companion to the book itself.

As to *The Theology of the Body*, there is a gifted author, Christopher West, who has broken down and explained the Holy Father's philosophy of human sexuality in conjunction with the Church's teachings on sexual morality in his outstanding book, *Good News About Sex and Marriage*. It is a priceless companion to understanding the practical applications of the Church's teachings on sex to everyday life.

This present chapter cannot encompass all that these authors have written, and written so well, on this important topic. You are directed to these much more articulate and authoritative authors to gain greater understanding of the majesty and beauty of the gift of sex that the Lord has placed in you, in me, and in every one of us.

What we are going to focus on here is the question: because your sexuality is a God-given part of you, what role does it play in the discernment of your spouse?

It plays an important role, as a matter of fact. But at the outset, we need to note that it's hard to actually define what sexual attraction is in the discernment process. Maybe it is best included under the category of "feelings and personal preferences." Some might call it a sign. Since it is so hard to categorize, it really deserves its own special treatment here. So let's start with some truths about sexual attraction.

Sexual attraction is a good thing. It is good and normal and natural to experience sexual attraction. God made us male and female, and He wants the human race to go on and continue. He sees to that by giving us the feeling of sexual attraction so that we will seek out mates, mate with them, and have offspring. Sexual attraction is intrinsically good, in and of itself, because God created it in us.

There is one person that you are definitely supposed to feel sexually attracted to, and that is your spouse.

163

The world has tried so much to vilify sex, to make it dirty, to make everyone feel filled with shame about sex. Even religious, devout people might get to the point of thinking that any sexual attraction is bad. Quite to the contrary, there is one person you are supposed to have these sexual feelings for, and that is your husband or wife. And those feelings don't just show up on your wedding night. They are present before marriage as well. That is why sexual attraction can be an important indicator of whether someone might be your chosen spouse. You should expect to feel intense sexual attraction when that person comes along.

Sexual attraction is very powerful and must be reined in, controlled, and considered wisely. There is no question that the power of the sexual urge is an extremely strong drive in us as human beings. Controlling this drive is one of the great struggles for all persons as they go through life, whatever their state in life. When you are presented with a person for whom you have strong sexual attraction, you have to really work to keep yourself in the driver's seat of your attraction and not let it take control or overtake your rational self. There will be this struggle, even if the person you are dating is called to be your spouse.

Sexual attraction is easily influenced by outside interferences, especially Satan. Satan is the prince of this world. He loves to pervert and twist around anything that is of God, and that includes sex. One need only look around this world, filled with Internet pornography, incest, child prostitution, teenage sex parties, and the like, to see how Satan profanes that which God intends to be holy. And Satan is certainly capable of influencing someone's sexual feelings as a way to usurp God's plans for you concerning selection of your spouse. Satan is not beyond tempting you with strong sexual feelings for someone who is definitely *not* the person God has selected for you.

If you have been living the teachings of the Church concerning chastity, sexual attraction will be a more

accurate indicator concerning the identity your spouse. If you have been given the great grace of chastity, have been living chastely in the single life, are able to control your sexual desire, your sexuality is "rightly ordered"—that is, in line with how God wants for you to be living it—when you do feel sexual attraction for a person, you need to really take note of it.

Your sexuality has to be in harmony with your spirituality for it to be a good indicator for discernment. If you are living unchastely, involved in sexual activity, masturbation, pornography, or sexual fantasy, then sexual attraction will not be a very reliable sign of who your spouse is, because you have confused your ability to use it as a gift, and to read the truth of it, because of such sins.

One of the reasons that premarital chastity is important to maintain is that you don't want to be tainted by lots of sexual experiences or stimulations so that when the *real and true* sexual attraction comes along that is God-given and "heaven sent," i.e., with your potential spouse, you are not so anesthetized sexually that you can't recognize him or her. You don't want to be so numbed from all your earlier sexual experiences that you mistake just another case of the "hots" for "the exclamation." Nor do you want to mistake it the other way around and miss your spouse because you just want to have sex with almost anyone, and when your spouse does come along, he or she does not even register with you as anything special. Either way will not be helpful in true discernment.

But if you have been living chastely, and if there is a devout Catholic man or woman in your life that you like, you seem well-suited to, and they like you too, and you both have a sexual attraction to each other, you would be foolish not to give very serious consideration as to whether this is the person to whom God has called you for the vocation of marriage.

With these things in mind, how does one explore a sexual attraction to a certain person for purposes of discernment, that is, the gathering of information, looking for God's will in the situation?

First of all, the gathering of information on your sexual attraction to a person is not a license for immorality. Nothing here is advocating that any unchastity occur between you and the person you are dating. Don't misinterpret; sexual attraction is something you feel, it is not something you do. You need to get that straight from the start.

Never forget that your body is a temple of the Holy Spirit. Your boyfriend's or girlfriend's body is also a temple of the Holy Spirit. Will you violate that sanctity? It is rather like the Jewish temple, in which there were only certain people worthy of entering the holy of holies, the inner chamber of the temple. That is what sex is like. There is one high priest who is sanctioned to enter the temple of a person's body, and that is the person's spouse. If you are not that person's spouse (even if you are not yet that spouse, even if you intend to be and maybe even someday will be), you are not sanctioned to enter into that temple until marriage. Chastity must always be the standard and the goal sincerely strived for.

So how can you discern about your sexual attraction?

Have a frank conversation about your sexual histories. The way to begin is by talking. This is not to say you engage in salacious, sexy talk about how hot you are for each other. No, this is talking about sex the way mature adults discuss such a holy and important topic.

If you are cringing at the very thought of talking about sex with your partner, that's a real sign that you are not ready to get married, or that this is not the right person. If you are thinking about marriage with this person, you not only should be able to talk about sexual matters frankly, you should want to; you should welcome the opportunity to share these things with this one person, if they are the person with whom you are meant to live the sacrament of marriage.

If you have been following along with these guidelines, you and your partner have long ago had a discussion about abortion and birth control, and the Church's teachings on those topics. As you date more and get to know each other better, it is time to start talking about the more intimate topics of sexuality.

The best place to start is with sharing the general details of your sexual history. You will know when the time is right for such a conversation, but be mindful that it probably will be necessary earlier than you might first think. If the relationship is at a point where "the world" would not be surprised if the two of you were sexually involved (you are dating, spending lots of time together, have had romantic physical contact), then that means temptation is also present, and it's time to be honest about the situation and where you find yourselves in this relationship.

You need to share with your partner, and he or she with you, whether you are still virgins, whether you have saved the gift of your sexuality for your spouses. That might be a difficult statement for you to make, or for your partner to make, but if you truly care about each other, you will want to share this information.

You need to have a frank conversation about your sexual pasts, eliciting information like: Are you a virgin? If you are not a virgin, how old were you when you first had sexual intercourse? What were the general circumstances? How many sex partners have you had? When was the last time you had sex with someone? What were the circumstances of the relationships where you engaged in sex? Was contraception a part of those relationships? Were any children born of (or conceived in) those sexual relationships? Are you "technically" a virgin but have engaged in other sexual activities (such as manual stimulation to orgasm or oral sex)?

Ultimately, you and your partner would need to discuss whether you had been involved with abortion, and whether either of you had any sexually transmitted diseases (syphilis, gonorrhea, chlamydia) or suffer from any now (HIV, genital warts, herpes).

You need to talk about how these experiences have affected you sexually, your faith walk, and your current understanding of why you allowed these sins into your life. Talk about how you feel about the situations now. What are your regrets? What did you learn? How do you view it all now?

Christopher West speaks of a concept best described as premarital infidelity. This idea suggests that because there is a spouse out there somewhere for you, every sexual act outside of your eventual union with that one person was an act of infidelity against him or her, even if you didn't know the person yet. If this is a person with whom you are discerning possible marriage, recounting your sexual past is a very important step. You tell him or her about these earlier transgressions and ask for forgiveness, because you were in essence being unfaithful to him or her, to the vows that you would one day make in marriage (West, p. 101).

While our faith requires only that a person confess such sins to a priest in the sacrament of reconciliation, this kind of self-revelation can be very healing and unifying in a relationship that is perhaps leading to marriage.

No one is perfect. All have fallen short of the glory of God, and all have sinned. You need to approach each other with forgiving and understanding hearts, and show each other the same mercy that you hope they will show to you. But this could be a very profound step for both of you. Does this person feel like someone whom you should be asking for forgiveness for your past sexual liaisons? That would be an indication that he or she is your spouse.

Perhaps this will be a very short conversation. Maybe you have both saved yourself for marriage and have been completely chaste in your single life. What a beautiful thing in our modern world that would be. The Beatitudes tell us, "Blessed are the pure in heart, for they shall see God" (Matt.

5:8). Rejoice in the gift of chastity God has placed in each of you, and ask for His continued grace to live in such holiness as you grow together as a couple. Two Catholic virgins, at any age, finding each other in this world is practically a miracle in itself, and could be a strong sign that God may be calling the two of you to the sacrament of marriage. A union between you would certainly be a testimony to His grace and mercy, wouldn't it?

Or it might be that each of you has a lot of sexual history, and there is a lot to talk about. Take the time to do so, as hard as it might be. Your future might depend on it, so be honest and open now. If this person is perhaps going to be your spouse, you can have no secrets, especially in matters that concern the sanctity of the marriage bed.

There is a great expression: "Water seeks its own level." The idea is that water, when it runs off, always seeks to be at sea level. That is a good metaphor for people joining in marriage as well, particularly when it comes to sexual experience.

Perhaps the best sexual yoke is an equal yoke: virgin with virgin, the sexually experienced with the sexually experienced. For one person to be a virgin and the other to have extensive sexual experience is a struggle at best, and a disaster waiting to happen at worst. While it's hoped that maybe one's greater experience with chastity will help the other live the charism more fully now, the more likely scenario is that the more sexually experienced person could draw the more chaste into sin. That is what Satan is banking on.

After a certain age, many people will have had some sexual experiences, and probably beyond that, it becomes a matter of degree. What is more important than the past, however, is the present. That is the next step of the conversation.

Talk about your current chastity convictions. You need to talk about your current personal convictions concerning chastity. If you have been chaste, is that because you are committed to it, or has there just not been a present opportunity to engage in sexual sin? How do you control your sexual desires now that they have a living, breathing context, i.e., with the person you are now dating?

If you have been sexually active in the past, what has been your history lately for abstinence and chaste living? How long has it been since you engaged in sexual activity? How have you been able to live chastely as a single person? You each need to share the answers to these kinds of questions if you are to have any hope of having the kind of intimate and loving relationship that is called for in the sacrament of marriage.

Exactly what are your chastity convictions now? What are your partner's? That is what will determine whether this relationship will go on and whether you might be called to the vocation of marriage together. This is of the utmost importance. You each must tell the other what you believe concerning premarital chastity and how you live that belief. The Church teaches that premarital sexual intercourse is a sin. The Church teaches that contraception is a sin. The Church teaches that sexual immorality (which would include any sexual activity that can lead to orgasm) and fornication (sexual union between unmarried persons) are sins. The Church teaches that masturbation is a sin. So what do you believe and do? What does he or she believe and do?

Unless your partner believes and is seriously trying to live all that the Church espouses, here is the bottom line: they are probably not God's chosen spouse for you. It is in this conversation that the rubber meets the road, so to speak. There are all kinds of people out there in the Catholic Church who think that intercourse is fine if you love each other, if you are engaged, if you are getting married eventually anyway. That is not what the Church teaches. "The sexual act must take place exclusively within marriage. Outside of marriage it always constitutes a grave sin and excludes one from sacramental communion" (Catechism, para. 2390).

There are Catholics who think that, well, okay, we won't have intercourse, but we will have oral sex, or stimulate each other manually to orgasms; we will do "everything but" and that is okay. That is not what the Church teaches. Fornication is the "carnal union between an unmarried man and an unmarried woman. It is gravely contrary to the dignity of persons and of human sexuality" (Catechism, para. 2353).

There are Catholics who think that using birth control pills, condoms, diaphragms, IUDs, and other artificial contraception is perfectly acceptable. That is not what the Church teaches. "'Every action which, whether in anticipation of the conjugal act, or in its accomplishment, or in the development of its natural consequences, proposes, whether as an end or as a means, to render procreation impossible' is intrinsically evil" (Catechism, para. 2370).

There are Catholics who think that you can neck all you want, get very sexually turned on, and then go home and masturbate to relieve your sexual tension, and think that is okay, just as long as you aren't "doing it" together. That is not what the Church teaches. "Masturbation is an intrinsically and gravely disordered action" (Catechism, para. 2352).

Your sexual attraction might have drawn you together, but if these kinds of things are what you are finding out from your partner, this is not the person for you, if they don't believe in and aspire to the Church's teachings.

This is the bottom line: God is going to send you someone who complements you sexually. You will be attracted to them, and they will be attracted to you. But God is not going to send someone who will try to compromise your chastity with sin. God will not send you someone who wants to use contraception in married life or who wants either of you to use it premaritally. If you are dating someone and the conversation gets to this point, and you learn this is what they believe, it is time to say good-bye, or at most be friends, because this is not the partner God has planned for you. You might want to advise that they get greater instruction on these important aspects of the faith, but they are not (at least at this point) the person God has chosen for your spouse.

God will not send you someone who wants you to sin sexually. Nor will He send someone who would think of compromising your immortal soul by engaging in any act of unchastity or immorality with you. He will not send someone with whom, in loving them, you are tempted beyond control to do these things yourself.

The situation you hope to find from these conversations is that whatever someone's sexual past, they now embrace fully the Church's teachings on sex and have committed to living them out, and living them in your relationship in particular. If that is who you are involved with, you are well on your way to a good discernment, because both of your hearts are in the right place.

If these conversations continue, you will eventually get to how you plan to manage your sexuality within the context of marriage in general. At this point, if you are still discerning, you should both be committed to never using artificial contraception in any marriage between you. That means that you should talk about natural family planning (NFP), which the Church allows as a means of spacing children in marriage, if there are legitimate reasons to do so. NFP involves observing and recording the woman's bodily changes (mainly temperature and vaginal secretion changes) to determine the time of ovulation so that the couple can choose to abstain from sexual activity during the fertile phases to possibly space the conception of children. You can talk about this important subject too.

It is a good idea for NFP monitoring to begin before marriage. The woman has practice with and some history of charting in place so that NFP will be as effective as possible when the time comes in marriage to use it fully. While this is probably more of an activity for an engaged couple, it is appropriate in the course of serious dating to learn more and discuss this important topic.

You might want to study some of this together. Maybe you can get the *Theology of the Body* or *Love and Responsibility* books and read them together as a couple. Read the Catechism together on sex and marriage and discuss it. Read and discuss *Good News About Sex and Marriage*. That might help give a context to some of these more difficult sexual topics.

If you are balking at the very idea of this—that there is no way you can talk about all this with your partner—your answer was just made simple: you are not called to marriage, not now, not with this person. You *have* to be able to talk frankly like this, and if you can't, you are in no position to get married.

At this point, you will have learned a lot about your partner's sexual past, their commitment to chastity now, and their understanding and interest in honoring their sexuality, both premaritally and in marriage. Armed with all this knowledge, if you still want to go forward together, you are going to need a plan.

Create a "chastity plan" together. The Catechism teaches that chastity is "an *apprenticeship in self-mastery* which is a training in human freedom" (Catechism, para. 2339). This is what you are both doing, seeking self-mastery of your sexuality in the context of your relationship. To do that, you need a plan as to how you will navigate your way into true freedom by having a chaste and loving relationship.

What you need is a carefully thought-out "chastity plan" that both of you can commit to. You don't wait to talk about these things until you are in the heat of a "make out" session, that is for sure. This is a mature conversation that you have when heads are cool and hearts are in the right place.

Knowing each other's sexual pasts is very important in crafting your plan. While someone might be committed to chastity now, if they have a sexual past from which they learned what sex is all about, they know what they are missing, in a sense. It is very hard to put that "genie" back in the bottle, shall we say. Keeping things in check is going to be difficult. So if you are going to be a couple together, navigating these sexually charged waters, you really need a concrete plan you both understand, agree to, and can live out joyfully and faithfully.

The first principle for your plan has to be, don't "tow the line," and by that we mean, just keep exploring, experimenting, pushing the sexual envelope, and flirting with sexual disaster. Satan would like nothing better than to cause two people that God has called to the sanctity of holy matrimony to commit sexual sins together. Satan loves that: he takes down two souls for the price of one. There is such economy of effort for him in doing that—it is a no-brainer on his part. So he will certainly tempt the two of you to sin sexually, no matter how holy your calling together might be.

Outside of marriage, it is immoral to engage in any touching or kissing whose primary purpose is preparation of either party for sexual intercourse. Here is that sentence again: it is immoral to engage in any touching or kissing whose primary purpose is preparation of either party for sexual intercourse. If that is what you are doing, stop it immediately and come up with a chastity plan that is in conformity with Church teaching.

For some couples, no intimate physical contact at all is the plan that works for them. Even in this day and age, there are couples who do not even kiss until after they are pronounced man and wife at their wedding. While that may sound archaic to our modern way of thinking, what a beautiful testimony it is to the strength of the virtue of chastity. If God has given the two of you the charism of chastity to such an extent, this could be your chastity plan. For most people, this would be very difficult, but this kind of heroic virtue is indeed possible, with God's grace.

Most couples will devise a chastity plan that includes kissing and touching, but to what extent and in what circumstances? The goal here is to gain control and self-mastery, as the Catechism says. Some couples try to avoid all near occasions of sin in the sense that they plan to never be alone together so that they are not tempted too much in their interactions. And that is a good plan. Just make sure that you live it with an acknowledgment of the dignity of your sexuality. We are not dogs, tied up on chains of restraint and the only reason we do not sin sexually is because we never had the opportunity. To think of it in that manner denigrates the dignity of your sexuality. You want to be chaste together because you chose to be, not because you didn't have the chance *not* to be.

What you are striving for in a chastity plan is giving back to the Lord the gift of your restraint and your waiting for His time when the full expression of your sexuality can be realized, that is, in marriage. How pleasing it is to the Lord when we choose to abstain and choose chastity in the face of a clear and present opportunity and desire to have sex.

Abstinence actually is a form of sexual expression, perhaps the most highly evolved form. By abstaining from premarital sexual activity, you are honoring the dignity of your sexuality and that of your partner in a way that is very pleasing to God, as it is in accordance with His will and His moral law. What better ideal to express to the person the Lord has brought to you to possibly be your spouse?

Some chastity plans might do well to just have some kind of "bright line" rule, such as, nothing more than kissing from the neck up. No hands anywhere but on the arms, back, or shoulders. No unfastening or removing clothes. No nudity. No spending the night together because we're "just sleeping." No vacations alone together, or weekends at each other's places without others around. Some couples do well with rules like that.

Some couples might be able to have a chastity plan that could be called "the swimsuit rule": no touching or kissing any place that would be covered up by swimsuits worn at a normal American (not topless!) beach. This could mean that hands, feet, arms, legs, backs, shoulders, stomachs, and the man's chest, would be fair territory for caressing and kissing. A great deal of sensuality could be involved in this, and for some, it would be too tempting and too stimulating, and therefore immoral. But for some people, perhaps more mature couples with a lot of learned and conditioned sexual restraint, this plan might work and not lead to any immortality.

Really, anything beyond what has been described above would take you into the realm of touching or kissing whose primary purpose is to prepare one or the other of you for sexual intercourse, and therefore you cannot morally engage in such further activities.

One place where couples get into trouble is in not drawing a "bright line" at the woman's breasts. You know in your heart that touching and kissing a woman's bare breasts is really done for one purpose and one purpose only: sexual arousal. For some women, this kind of contact is very arousing. For almost all men, seeing, touching, and kissing a woman's breasts is extremely arousing (remember, the guideline is whether the activity's primary purpose is to prepare *either* of you for intercourse). As inviting as that kind of contact might seem, it is probably immoral.

People have a pretty inherent sense of what is right and wrong when it comes to sex, if they are honest with themselves. Would you want your parents or your parish priest to walk in on what you are doing? If not, that is a pretty good idea of what you should not be doing.

Even if there is no touching involved, there can still be immorality. For example, nudity is not immoral on its own. The human body is a good and beautiful thing. But seeing each other naked, even without any touching, would still be a sin against chastity. It is immodest, violates the sanctity of the body as a temple of the Holy Spirit, and it leaves in the mind of your partner images that would likely become part of sexual fantasy, great temptation, and the near occasion of sin for them. Nudity then becomes a sin against charity as well.

Or what about the situation where everyone is fully clothed, no hands or kisses are being employed, but you are rolling around all over each other, with movement, body weight, or pressure on each other's bodies, including the genitals? This kind of indirect stimulation can be as arousing as manual or oral genital stimulation. So just because nobody's hands or kisses are straying into the "red zones," the activity could still be illicit.

You need to be mindful that even if your plan is set up in terms of body "geography" (such as, not "south" of this border), that does not mean that your touching and kissing in "safe territory" still might not cross the line into sin. Even kissing on the lips, if it is intended for the purpose of preparing either party for sexual intercourse, can become sinful. Some people's mouths and necks are very erogenous, and even kissing them there (which should seem chaste enough) can be very sexually arousing. To persist in necking and kissing in that situation can become sinful. It depends on the individual, and that is why you need communication and a plan adapted to the particulars of your own situation.

What about sexual conversation? There is nothing immoral in talking about sex in the manner which we are setting forth here. The kind of frank conversation espoused here is going to be essential and required if you are going to have a chaste courtship. But what about sexually stimulating conversation, the purpose of which is to arouse your partner or yourself? Any conversation that is purely sexual fantasy that involves what you would like to do to each other sexually is probably immoral. To have late-night phone calls, pillow talk, that goes beyond your wishes to be together, or that you miss holding each other, or you wish you could kiss her right now—if it goes much beyond that, into vivid descriptions of sexual activities you wish you could be engaging in but can't, you are going too far. In an interplay of the sixth and ninth commandments, if you can't do it licitly under the sixth commandment, then you ought not be talking about it, or dwelling on it, under the ninth commandment.

To engage in acts or conversations that overstimulate your partner such that they are so sexually aroused to the point of physically hurting, or being tempted to relieve themselves with the sin of masturbation, is a terrible thing to do to someone you care about. It is a sin against charity. You do not want to do that to them, and they should not want to do that to you.

Why are all these specifics necessary? If the depth of your sexual and spiritual integration has been "Well, the Church says I can't so I just won't," that is a good enough plan that works fairly well when you are not in a relationship with someone you love and care about and want to have sex with. But now you are going to need a whole new level and depth of understanding of the gift of your sexuality to live out chastity in a relationship where sex would have a part, once you would be joined in the sacrament of marriage.

The place you want to get to is that, with the person who is to be your spouse, you won't really even *consider* engaging in sexual activity with them any way other than the way God intended for you two to have it: uncontracepted vaginal intercourse in your marriage bed. God will give you the grace to desire that, and only that. Any acts less than that (petting, manual stimulation, masturbation, oral sex, contracepted and/or premarital intercourse) are all counterfeit experiences of the fullness of the sexual expression God has called you to.

Think of it with this analogy. A man studying for the priesthood may really want to say Mass, and preach, and anoint the sick, but if he were to try to do these things before he has received holy orders, what he would be doing is a sham. Any sexual activity before a sacramental marriage is like that, a woefully inadequate counterfeit of the real joy of sacramental sex.

Similarly, in the Catholic Church we have Christ's true Body and Blood in the Eucharist. If you know that is waiting for you, why would you want to go to a Communion service at a non-Catholic church and have just crackers and grape juice? There is no point to it. That is what premarital sexual activity is like. Just hold out for the real thing. You will be glad you did.

It's natural that you want to show affection and give each other pleasure and comfort and have intimacy; that is what the Church calls the "unitive" function of marriage that you both may feel drawn to. But every sexual act must also carry with it the "procreative" function of love as well. Unless and until you are free to have vaginal intercourse—the marital embrace—in a situation sanctioned by God (namely, in the sacrament of marriage), you will never be fully open to both the unitive and procreative ends you are called to.

When it comes to crafting your chastity plan, keep in mind that all the touching and intimacy in your relationship should be for the "higher purposes." By that we mean it must be exclusive, charitable, loving, and for the other person's greatest good, and that is always in reference to their dignity as a child of God, in reference to their immortal soul. When you are sitting on the couch in the dark, kissing, you hold your partner's soul in your hands. Be a good steward of it. You are looking for the person who is going to put your soul first, over and above their own physical pleasure—the person who would sooner die than compromise your soul. That is who you are looking for when you are discerning from your sexual attraction.

Living out the virtue of chastity together in your relationship. Now that you have a chastity plan, how are you going to make it work? This is where that "speed dating" technique of communal examination of conscience might really help you (see Chapter 6). If you have a chastity plan, you are not going to want to confess any violation of it, are you? This is a way to help each other stay on the straight and narrow pathway.

As part of effectuating your chastity plan, make a vow of chastity, each to the other, that you will never do anything to him or her, or let them do to you, anything that is contrary to what the Church teaches is appropriate. Giving your word to someone can be a powerful experience and might really help you in times of temptation. Whether your partner is willing to make such a promise will tell you a lot for your discernment.

Another thing to do to help your chastity is to make going to Mass a part of your times together. If you know you are going to be receiving the Lord in the Holy Eucharist later on, there is much less likelihood you will engage in any immoral sexual activity. It is a good safeguard, so use it.

You might make a visit to a perpetual adoration chapel a part of your dates. Again, knowing that you will be together in the presence of the Lord Himself later on will keep a very tight rein on any sexual temptation in your relationship.

Pray together. That should almost go without saying. You might particularly want to place the chastity of your relationship under the protective mantle of the Blessed Virgin Mary. Who better than the Mother of God, who was blessed with the gift of perpetual virginity and perfect chastity, to help the two of you? Perhaps you can use the Hail Mary or even a Marian prayer that you write together as your special weapon to fight off strong temptation. It should be something you both can call upon and say easily in the midst of your times together when temptation starts to come on strong. What a beautiful thing if in the midst of sexual temptation, the two of you would stop what you are doing and pray for help in controlling yourselves and your desires. The person who will do this with you could well be someone who could be your holy spouse.

You both might also want to use blessed sacramentals as a reminder of your commitment to chastity. The wearing of a scapular, cross, crucifix, or religious medals around the neck can be a very powerful reminder that your and your partner's bodies are temples of the Holy Spirit. In a romantic session, if your partner's religious medals are jangling in the midst of your touching, or if your kisses come upon the chain of her necklace on which hangs the image of Christ on the cross, these are pretty hard to ignore, and might be just the kind of reminders you need to stay on track.

You also might want to enlist the aid of persons close to you to help the two of you stay true to your convictions. While your chastity plan is very private between the two of you, if you live with family or roommates, you might want to share that the two of you want to have a chaste relationship (that is all they need to know). If you know you have "witnesses" who are mindful of your comings and goings and your activities, it might help to keep the two of you accountable. Of course, ultimately you are responsible for yourselves, but if your roommate knows you are trying to live chastely, won't it be harder to face her in the morning if you didn't come home the night before?

On the point of other people, you both must be careful about the sin of scandal, that is, doing anything that might lead others into sin. That comes with things like spending the night together, even if it is perfectly chaste between the two of you. Why? Because no one else will believe you that "nothing happens" when you are alone like that together. If you have younger brothers and sisters, or have friends or roommates who are not in the Church, and if they know that you two proclaim to be devout Catholics but see you acting in a manner that suggests one can still be "holy" and do things that *look* as though you are sinning, they think they can do it too. But in actuality, they would likely sin if they were in the same situation. That is the "sin of scandal" because you might lead those others into sin by your example. So, no spending the night at each other's place, or going on vacation alone together, or getting one hotel room because "it's cheaper"—things like that. That can lead to the sin of scandal, and that is not the Christian witness the two of you want to be. What kind of testimony to the Gospel are the two of you being? Your marriage is supposed to be an example to the world on how to live the Gospel. If you might be called to marriage, why not start being that example now?

Discerning in your chaste sexual relationship. We are talking a lot here about what to do in your relationship as far as chastity is concerned, but what does it all mean to discerning if this is the person for you?

First of all, if your partner does not want to have these kinds of conversations, and does not want to devise a chastity plan with you, your discernment is pretty easy: they are not the person for you. God will not send you someone who does not honor your sexuality and your chastity convictions. If your partner is balking at the idea of all of this, you have already discerned what you need to know: they are not "the one."

But if your partner is willing to do all this, as you live your chastity plan together, you will get much information for further discernment. Your exercises in chastity will reveal to you whether your partner can control himself or herself. Your spouse has to have self-control. There are many situations in marriage where chastity and abstinence are required. There are times during pregnancy, illness, or absence, that a couple cannot engage in the marital embrace. There would also be those times of abstinence if you employ NFP. You need to see now if your partner has this kind of self-control. If they can't do it with you now, what makes you think that, after marriage, they are going to have any better control when you are not available to them sexually?

It's been said that appropriate kissing and touching is training in heroic virtue. That is completely true. Just ask any devout Catholic couple that is called to the vocation of marriage, engaged, and just waiting for their marriage to begin. Talk about heroic virtue! But God will reward that kind of fidelity.

You are probably thinking, how can you discern your sexual attraction if you can't "do" anything sexually? Quite to the contrary, you can discern a whole lot about someone doing nothing.

You discern with your eyes, first of all. Do you love the way the person looks—their eyes, their face, their smile, the way they radiate back at you? That is attraction. Do you love their overall shape, the way their body fits together, how they move, the way they fill their space? That is attraction.

Without even touching, do you like being close to them? Do you find yourself leaning in, moving closer, just to be nearer to them? Do you feel an energy when you are near them? That is attraction.

When you do touch, whether it is holding hands, walking arm-in-arm, cuddling, or chaste kissing, does your stomach do flips, do you tremble, do you get kind of goofy (what I call "the stupids"), as if you can't even talk, you are so flustered just being touched by this person? That is *really* attraction. See, you can feel sexual attraction without engaging in anything immoral. And you can draw conclusions from that attraction as well.

Chastity allows you to get past the lust and really see and appreciate the whole of your partner's sexuality. Ultimately, sexual attraction must draw you not just to the sexual act but to the whole of the other person's sexuality, which includes their fertility, their ability to procreate. That is a very important part of the discernment of sexual attraction.

Part of what you are really discerning about this person is whether they are to be the father or mother of your children, should God send that blessing to you. What you should be connecting to, if you are called together, is the entirety of your partner's sexuality, the complete expression of their femaleness or maleness, which includes their fertility. A major reason for marriage is procreation, so fertility cannot be separated from your partner's sexuality.

For the women, when you see this man, do you see more than a sexy physique, his suave manner, and a seductive style? Do you see him as the man you want to share your fertility with, conceive with, give over your body for nine months to nurture his baby inside you, have him there as you struggle through 24 hours of labor, giving birth to his baby? Do you want to have him there when you breastfeed that baby? And have him be daddy to your precious children? Because that is what all this sexual attraction is really pointing to, if you are called to the sacrament of marriage together.

For the men, are you connecting just to her shapely body, how she looks in a swimsuit, and how jealous all your buddies will be when they see you with her? What this is really about, if you are called together, is the whole of her feminine sexuality, which includes hormonal cycles, ovulation, menstruation, conception, gestation, childbirth, and lactation. She is more than a source of pleasure for you, she is more than a receptacle, more than an object, more than the lust of your eye. That is where sexual attraction should be leading you, to the whole of her sexuality, if you are called to the sacrament of marriage together.

Christopher West suggests that sacramental marital sex has a message, and it should be something like this: "I love you totally, completely, all that you are, with all that I am. I give myself freely and totally to you." Anything other than that says "I love you *but* . . ." (West, p. 108). "I love you, but not that part of you which can make me pregnant." Or "I love you, but not if I have to know anything about your periods." Or "I love you, but not enough to raise a baby with you." That is when sex becomes a sham and not at all what God intended for it to be. If your partner's actions or beliefs, as revealed by this process, are really saying, "I love you but . . . ," he or she is not the person God is sending.

As you go along and continue dating, and walk this sexual path together, it will get harder and harder not to want to consummate your relationship, but don't. You would be cheating yourselves out of what God really has in store for you. Don't be chaste during your courtship and then get engaged and have sex because "you are getting married anyway." If you are going to do that (besides its being a sin), what was all this waiting for? No, make this commitment to be chaste into your marriage. You will never regret that decision.

The Bible says that it is better to marry than to burn with passion (1 Cor. 7:7). If you are called to marriage together, don't put it off for too long. There will be greater and greater temptation, and Satan would be so happy to make the two of you sin sexually on the eve of the sacrament of marriage. Don't let him tempt you that way by planning some big wedding that is years off. Better to marry sooner, and simply, than to commit any sexual sin together.

There is a wonderful organization called the Couple to Couple League, which is an international Catholic organization that promotes NFP. They have great information, and you are strongly encouraged to contact them, visit their Web site, and order their materials on sexuality in marriage as well as on NFP. A point they make is that in NFP, when a couple is abstaining from intercourse during the fertile times, the couple might have trouble with that and want to give in and have intercourse. They can do that, of course, as it is their privilege of marriage.

But the point made is that if a couple thinks they want to space their children, and are trying to abstain but are having great difficulty doing so, maybe that is God actually calling them to have a child, now. That is an interesting concept—that a strong urge to sexual union might be God calling them together to conceive.

There is an analogy that can be drawn in premarital sexual attraction as well. If a couple is discerning marriage, and is strongly drawn to each other sexually, that could be the call of the Holy Spirit as well, not prompting them to sin premaritally but to get themselves married, because He has a new life that He wants to bring forth by their union together—as if the Holy Spirit is standing by (perhaps a bit impatiently), waiting to bring life forth through the two of you.

So feeling that you want to break down is not necessarily a bad sign for purposes of discernment. While you can't succumb to it (unlike that already married couple), the urge for sexual union with this person could mean something very profound—that the Holy Spirit is calling you together into the fruitfulness of marriage.

Sexual attraction is an important "sign" in the discernment of the call to marriage. Sex speaks the language of forever; there is an eternal quality about sex because it is so imbued with God and the mystery of His creativity, and He allows us to share in that in the sacrament of marriage. Foremost, you are looking for the person who fully understands and embraces the sacramental expression of the gift of human sexuality in marriage.

By talking about sex in a full and frank manner, sharing your past and current struggles where sex is concerned, and devising and living a shared chastity that honors God and the gift of sexuality He has placed in each of you, you should find some very good indicators of God's will for you concerning the call to marriage together. God can and will speak to you through the beautiful language of your body, and your partner's body, if you are called to be husband and wife.

Chapter 10

The Triangle

There is a wonderful book called *I Married You*, written by a Protestant pastor, Walter Trobisch. It is a treatise on Christian love and marriage. From that book, which I read as a young girl, I got an image of the triangle as having an application to love and marriage. Trobisch uses this geometric form to talk about the dynamic tension among the three areas of love, sex, and marriage. It was from that exposition that another idea came to me, about the triangle as a symbol for the sacrament of marriage.

The triangle is a fitting image for the relationship that gives rise to the sacrament of marriage because marriage is a covenant with God. It is a promise, a vow, you make, not only to your spouse, but also to God. It's a three-way promise and commitment. That is why the triangle is a wonderful symbol for the covenant and sacrament of marriage.

The triangle represents the interaction between God, man, and woman as they discern the vocation of marriage. God is the top point of the triangle. The man is the left point, and the woman the right point. The left side of the triangle is the man's relationship to God. The right side of the triangle is the woman's relationship to God. The bottom side of the triangle is the man's and woman's relationship to each other. Here's the illustration:

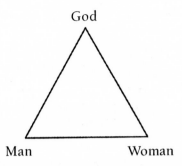

The triangulation of the relationship between God, man, and woman is there even before marriage. Before marriage, there is a relationship with God for each person, and there is also the relationship to each other. Discerning the vocation of marriage in part involves reading and interpreting this triangle, that dynamic three-way relationship between the two of you, and each of you with God.

This interaction of the three of you should be an equilateral triangle, that is, the length of the distances between each of the points should be the same, and should be maintained as a constant. With God as the apex, the man and woman are the two bottom angle points. In this world, the man and woman who are discerning the vocation of marriage are ever drawing toward each other, spiritually, emotionally, and sexually. Each is also reaching up to God, and God is reaching back to each of them. There is an equilibrium in all that reaching, an equistasis, you might call it, that needs to be maintained with an equal force, an equal pace, and an equal emphasis, for the harmony of the triangle to be maintained with its equal angles and distances. When these energies are all in harmony, the angles are equal, the sides are equal, and the triangle maintains its perfectly balanced shape.

Symbolically, if a couple is committed to the call of a

sacramental marriage, this geometry will be maintained. You need to be constantly "reading" the triangle the two of you have with God to see and discern how things are going.

Too often, trouble sets in if the couple has sex. As the world would see it, that would be the couple drawing closer together (the "unitive" aspect of marriage, some would argue). But as the couple draws closer in that regard, and the "line" between them gets shorter in the triangle, the whole triangle is thrown off. The bottom line is really short (the man and woman "close" together), and the relative lines to God getting farther and farther away, because of the sin that has entered the relationship. Like this:

God

Man   Woman

Or perhaps the woman is drawing closer to the man emotionally, and he is just staying where he is at out of fear of intimacy or commitment. Her "point" is moving closer to him, but he is static. The triangle turns into something approaching a right-angled triangle, and upsets the harmony that the three-part relationship should have. Like this:

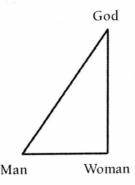

God

Man   Woman

Sometimes in all the excitement over each other, the man or the woman or both start to ignore their lines to God, and those lines start getting longer and longer, they are getting more distant from God as they get more involved in the worldly pursuit of each other and a life together. This changes the angles too, and sets the triangle off kilter. While God is constant, we are the variables in this triangulation, and that is not the perfect balance God intends:

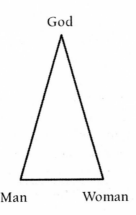

God

Man   Woman

A relationship that is on the course to a holy marriage is one in which the man is reaching for the woman on all levels the same as she is reaching for him, and they are both reaching up to God equally and fervently. The triangle has harmony and integrity, and maintains a perfect equilateral shape.

That is the image that should be in place for you to enter into marriage. This is the form to which you need to compare your relationship to see if you are on track. Are you both equally close to God and to each other? Are you as close to the other person as he or she is to you? Has no level of the relationship gone past what God has ordained is moral and right, such as your sexual relationship? Have all levels of the relationship gone as far as God is calling you, to gather information, so that full knowledge and discernment are present for you both? That is where you need to be to be thinking about committing to marriage.

The symbol of the triangle shows its deeper meaning in what happens after the marriage ceremony. When a married couple consummates their marriage in the marital embrace—in that total giving of themselves to each other, making gifts of their lives, their bodies, and spirits, each to the other, in that total outpouring of self, that complete "yes" that is both unitive and procreative—they are making manifest the outward sign of the inward grace of the sacrament of marriage. When they do, something starts to happen to that triangle. You might say that a grace of the sacrament of marriage is that the triangle starts to contract, God drawing each spouse to Himself, each of them drawing themselves to Him (as each is now living the vocation they were called to, their way of salvation). The husband and wife are ever drawing the other nearer, and moving ever closer toward each other as only really happens after the full commitment is made, the union consummated, and the life together begun.

As that process goes on in a marriage, eventually there is no distance at all between husband and wife (as is so beautifully manifested in their one-flesh union), and God has drawn each so much to Himself, and each has drawn so close to God, that the triangle is really no longer a triangle at all. The lines have drawn nearer and nearer, the points of man, woman, and God have come closer and closer, the triangle has become smaller and smaller, until eventually, the triangle has contracted in on itself so much that it becomes like a single point, all three points converged into one. An ecstatic, triune point. What a beautiful metaphor for the sacrament of marriage.

Therefore, the sacrament of marriage becomes a revelation of God Himself. Marriage is a reflection of the Triune Godhead, three who are one. The sacrament of marriage reveals some of the deepest mysteries of God in this covenant union with Him.

That is where you want to be someday in the sacrament of marriage, with another person in an ecstatic, triune union with God. And you need to get there from where you are now. So you need to ask yourself, what is the shape of our triangle? Is one of us closer to God? Is one of us closer to the other while the other stays static or is pulling away? Have we come closer together as a couple at the expense of either of our relationships to God? Has sin entered into our relationship, making both of us further away from God?

Is this a person to whom I can draw ever closer, ever nearer, and still draw myself to, and reach for, God? Is this a person with whom I can experience that ecstatic union with God? Those are very good questions to ponder in discernment of a spouse.

Discerning the state of your triangle as you journey along with someone should really assist you in discerning whether you are called with that person to the sacrament of marriage.

Chapter II

Forty Key Questions

There comes a point when you have to ask yourself the hard questions. It makes no sense to keep going on and on because you haven't faced the truth of the situation in which you find yourself. The moment of truth, the moment of reckoning, has to come, and it first has to come inside your own heart.

You must recognize the magnitude of what you are thinking about here, the vocation of marriage. This is one of the great responsibilities of your life, selecting your spouse. The decision you are trying to make could be the best, or the worst, decision you ever make. It will affect not only your life but many other lives—the other person, the people you each might go on to be involved with or marry (if you discern you are not to marry), the children you will have (or not have). Remember, you are not called to this vocation alone, so you cannot take this analysis lightly.

If you have been doing this whole process, there comes a time when you should ask yourself the following questions. Read the question and go with the first answer that comes to you. Your first, uncensored response is probably the truth of what is in your heart.

1. Will he/she help you get to heaven?
2. Do you love him/her?

3. Are you in love with him/her?
4. Have you been dating long enough (at least a year)?
5. Is his/her happiness more important to you than your own?
6. Do you feel you know everything important about him/her?
7. Has he/she allowed you into every area of his/her life?
8. Have you welcomed him/her into every area of your life?
9. Do you feel that your life will never be right unless he/she is in it?
10. Do your thoughts always turn to him/her?
11. When you are apart, do you long to be with him/her?
12. Do you have unwavering faith in him/her?
13. Is your earthly priority to do things that help and please him/her?
14. Does he/she inspire you and make you want to be the best person you can be?
15. Do you feel free and safe to tell him/her everything about you, all that happens to you, both good and bad?
16. Do you want to please the people that are important to him/her, like family and friends?
17. Will he/she do what is best for your family—the two of you and your children—and not just for himself/herself?
18. Are you willing to alter or even sacrifice your personal goals and plans for him/her?
19. Can he/she delay gratification?
20. Can each of you provide for a family financially should it become necessary?
21. Will he/she be a good parent?
22. Do you want him/her to be the mother/father of your children?

23. Do you want to be the mother/father of his/her children?
24. Do you completely trust him/her with your heart, your soul, your money, your life, your children?
25. Is he/she responsible?
26. Does he/she have a purpose in life?
27. Is he/she capable of sexual self-control?
28. Are you ready and wanting to give your whole self, your body, fully to him/her in the marital embrace, without shame, without reservation?
29. Do you admire and respect him/her?
30. Do you feel validated, respected, and honored by him/her?
31. When you think of the future, do your plans include him/her?
32. Do you share the same vision about your lives?
33. When you think about a future life together, do you feel hopeful and empowered?
34. Can you say that the world is a better place to you just knowing he/she is in it?
35. Can he/she run a family with loving authority and tireless organization?
36. Is he/she appreciative and respectful of the differences between the sexes?
37. Are you honest and clear on what motivates you to want to be with him/her?
38. If you were seriously ill, would you want him/her to physically care for you?
39. As you lay dying someday, do you want his/her face to be the last thing you see before you go to be with the Lord?
40. Can you make a lifelong commitment to him/her without reservation, enter into a covenant with him/her, and with God?

In addition to all the work that has gone before this point

in the process of discernment, all of these questions should be answered by you with a "yes" if someone is the person that God is calling you to marry at this time. If that is what you just experienced, you know what to do. It's time to say "yes" to God and accept the gift He has given you in this person, and say "yes" as well to the call to the vocation of marriage He has placed on your heart.

If there are some questions that you could not say "yes" to, you need to pray about the issues raised by the questions. Are there things that you have done or are doing that don't permit you to say "yes"? Is there work that God needs to do on your heart for you to be able to say "yes"? Are there things that you need to talk about with your partner to see if you can get to "yes"? Are some of these areas you could say "yes" to only once you are married, but feel you have sufficient faith that you can get to "yes" on the issues with this person? These are all good questions to reflect on further.

There are also some hypothetical questions that you can ask yourself as well. Remember St. Ignatius's advice? Ask yourself, if you let this person go, will you be able to stand before the judgment of God someday in good faith and say that you did everything you could to discern whether they were the right person or not? Will you have any regrets on your deathbed about this decision? What would you tell someone else who came to you for advice with all this same information?

There is a saying: You don't marry the person you can live with; you marry the person you can't live without. While no one is advocating that you should be so dependent on someone that you don't think you could go on living without them, the point really is that you are probably called to marry the person if you can say that you really don't see your life as a happy, productive life of service to God if it does not include them.

You don't marry someone whom you can merely stand,

someone who is the least of the evils, or who will just "do." God has something much bigger than that planned for you, and if the person you are dating is someone you feel you are settling for, don't. Simply, don't. You must choose them and they must choose you. Otherwise you may be cheating each other out of what God really has in store for each of you.

Dietrich von Hildebrand, in *Marriage: The Mystery of Faithful Love*, states that "only one motive can be admitted as completely adequate for marriage: mutual love and conviction that this union will lead to the eternal salvation of both spouses" (von Hildebrand, p. 64). That is the ultimate question you must ask yourself. If you can say that you love the person and that being together is the way of salvation for both of you, you have discerned that this is the person with whom you are called to marriage.

You will "know" when you have no more questions. When you feel that all your questions, including these questions, have been answered, then you will know what to do.

Chapter 12

Communal Discernment:
Are We Called to Marriage Together?

After you have gone through the process of discernment on your own, it is time to talk to your partner. Presumably, he or she has been doing the same things you have concerning God's will as to what He wants for his or her life too. You are each individuals, with a separate life path. What you are discerning is whether it is God's will that those paths converge and be one shared way for the two of you together in marriage.

Your job so far has been to keep your eyes open to God's hand in your own life, to hearing His voice in your own situation, to see what He would have you do. Once you have reached a point of certitude about what that is (whatever it is), it's time to act, and talk to your partner about it.

If you have done everything this book has suggested, put in the time dating someone, put in the effort, put in the time in prayer, you should be in a position to make a heartfelt discernment on the person you are with. You will never be 100 percent certain. The only thing we can be 100 percent certain of is the dogmas of the Church. About everything else we will have some doubts. But you have to be sure enough to a moral certainty. In something as important as marriage, you have to have that level of certitude. If you don't, it means either you need more information, you need to do more discernment, or the person is not the one for you.

Once you think you have as much certitude as you can have, given the circumstances, it's time to talk to your partner. It is hoped that you have already taken some of the mutual steps to discernment, like spiritual direction together, a retreat for purposes of discerning marriage, or a fasting from one another. It's not a good idea to do a lot of discerning on your own if your partner is not doing any. To have a big conversation sprung on him or her about whether you are called to marriage together might come as a big surprise if he or she was not thinking on that wavelength.

There should come a time, though, if you both have seeking hearts, trying to find God's will for each of your lives, when you conduct what we will call a "communal discernment." That is a period when the two of you go through a process of sharing and discerning together what God would have you do.

As we saw earlier, marriage is a service vocation, and you are called to the sacrament with someone else. So you need assent, or agreement, from that person to participate in the sacrament of marriage. (The Church also gets a say in whether you are called to the sacrament of marriage, but that usually doesn't come up until after a couple is engaged.)

If you have been following these recommendations and suggestions, if the Church has an objection to a potential union between you, you probably are already aware of it, either through your exploration of Church teaching or spiritual direction with a priest. But if you are past that, what we now are focusing on is taking the 50 percent of the discernment process that God has entrusted to you, along with the 50 percent God has entrusted to your partner, and comparing your conclusions.

What if your discernment of your 50 percent is that you are not called together to marriage? Isn't that just the end of it—we are not called, end of story? That would be a foolhardy approach to take, particularly if you are dating a devout Catholic who in many ways is a excellent match for you. God may want to use the process of communal discernment with your partner to show you your solo discernment was off somehow. To just say, "Well, I have decided, we are not called," is arrogant and prideful, because it shows you are not open to error in your own discernment, and anyone can be wrong about just about anything when it comes to figuring out God's will. So even if your conclusion so far is that you two are not called together, you need to go through the entire process, if only to confirm what you think you have already discerned.

Green sets out a course for "communal discernment" that is a process for how a religious order or community discerns God's will and decides the direction for the community as a whole on an issue (Green, p. 177). This process has a wonderful application to discerning the married vocation, because what the two of you might be forming is your own community of faith in a marriage and family. The decision whether to marry would be the first community decision your "order" is going to make, so it makes sense to use this technique for discernment.

Green states that communal discernment involves first gathering the necessary information and formulating the question to be answered. Then there are alternating periods of prayer and the sharing of the insights gained during prayer on the pros and cons of the question at issue. Thereafter, each member of the community goes off for solitary prayer and to seek discernment (using the experiences of consolations and desolations) of what is the Lord's will in the matter. Then, when the members return together and share their own individual discernment, there must be unanimity concerning God's will. Only with the unanimous consent of all is the community's collective discernment valid (Green, p. 180).

The way to apply this to the discernment of marriage is

to come together for an intense time of sharing and talking about what you have each been seeing and experiencing concerning the relationship. You might want to write each other letters, because if your discernment has included religious experiences, signs, messages from God, or insights from Scripture, these things can sometimes be hard to explain orally to someone, even to someone who cares deeply about you. This is because with all such experiences there is skepticism and doubt. That is natural; it's human to doubt, and it's good to test things, to be skeptical. And it's very hard sometimes to put a religious experience into words, because words often seem inadequate, never fully capturing the depth of the experience for you. So if you write it out for your partner, you can take your time explaining it, you have a better chance of their understanding, and you won't be hurt if their natural skepticism shows through as they try to understand what you've explained.

It is important to share with each other your "raw material" of discernment. You need to share more than your conclusion. You can't just say "We aren't called together" to someone who is discerning the vocation of marriage with you. They deserve much, much more than that. You need to share experience by experience what has happened to you, and how you tested each experience. You each need to go, one at a time, and set out the whole discernment you went through. Tell him or her the circumstances of your life when he or she came in. Tell what you first felt when you met. Tell how you have prayed about your relationship, and how God has answered. Tell what your spiritual advisor has to say about the two of you. Tell what signs you have seen. Tell what the good and bad fruits, the consolations and desolations, have been. Show to your partner that you have done all the work of gathering the information, testing it, and discerning about it, so he or she can know that you did everything that God asks of us in discerning His will.

It's important that you not hold anything back. You really need to share everything that has happened, even if it might be hard to say or if it's not favorable to your conclusion. For example, if you are concluding you are called together to the vocation of marriage, and if there have been desolations, bad fruits, or negative signs that you might want to ignore, don't do that to your partner. Tell them the whole of your experiences. They deserve to know the whole story, the good and the bad. Your partner may see positive or negative implications in things you have not previously noted, so trust your partner to be another set of eyes and ears, and to be another discerning heart with you.

This is really the time to be absolutely honest with your partner, in a spiritual sense. If ever there was a time for honesty, it is now. You are both making life-altering decisions right now, and you each deserve to have all the information that you can.

What you may find as you try to tell these things to your partner is that you haven't gathered enough data. It may be in the retelling of it that you see you are making such an important decision on insufficient data. Or maybe in the retelling of it, something will jump out at you that you didn't see before that tells you some experience was not of God, or that you misread something along the way. Sometimes in just hearing yourself tell the whole story, you will start to feel doubt about your conclusion, or maybe have more certitude about your conclusion. Maybe God will use the process of telling your partner about your discernment to tell you that you are not yet done discerning yourself.

After each of you have had a turn setting out your raw data, it is time to take on the role of spiritual advisor, each to the other. Each person should objectively take the other's experiences and play "devil's advocate" and test the experiences. Perhaps your partner will see things in your experiences that you didn't. Maybe your partner can see the "tail of the snake" in an experience that you previously thought was from God, when it really was from Satan. Perhaps using their reason, your partner will see an explanation that you did not see, since we all have different intellectual gifts. This is a very vital step.

You might say, "I already went over everything with my spiritual advisor; why do I have to go through it again with my partner?" While the priest's objectivity is very valuable, your partner's firsthand experience of your shared experiences provides an insight that the priest would not have. Your partner was there and might have a recollection of parts of shared experiences you forgot about, or didn't focus on, or wanted to ignore, which could change the entire meaning of an experience for you from black to white, perhaps. So switching places, and letting your partner pick apart each of your items of data, is a very important step in the communal discernment process.

This is not about one of you being right, and who is better at discerning. We all need all the help we can get at discerning the will of God. If this is a person you have loved, trusted, shared your faith with, and whom you respect in the faith, who better to lay out for their review these intimate movements of your heart? And there is no one who more deserves to know and scrutinize your discernment. Either way, no one will be more affected by your discernment than this person. If you are discerning that you are called to marriage together, he or she needs to be assured of your sincerity, that you really are called and not just deciding based on some experience that really is not of God. If you have decided you are not called, that person deserves to know why not, example by example, and given the chance to test it for themselves, maybe so they can come around to your way of seeing things, or maybe because it will further support their own conclusion that they have reached too, that you are not called together. Either way, you each deserve the whole story, and the chance to test each chapter of that story.

This process will likely take some time, perhaps many

hours of talking and sharing. Take your time. This is much too important a decision to be made lightly, or without all the due reflection it deserves. This is not about first reactions. It is about listening, really hearing, testing, reflecting, and discussing. That takes time.

Ultimately, you each must reflect on what the other has had to say. You need to reflect on what telling your own discernment has made you feel about your 50 percent of the discernment. Are you still as convinced that your discernment was right in all its steps? You need to take to heart any critique or insights your partner offered about your 50 percent of the discernment. Does he or she make valid points that you had not considered before?

Perhaps the thing that needs the most reflection is thinking about and praying about what your partner had to tell you about his or her journey and discernment. You need to test your partner's data, and that might require some digesting of information.

You might have had no idea that your partner was having lots of answers to prayers, signs, insights, or guidance from a priest and family, about you and your relationship. It all might be news to you, and some of it perhaps is scary, or overwhelming, in some ways. That this person is so seriously considering you for the vocation of marriage can be a really deep revelation. So you each need a chance to think over what the other has had to say, in private and in prayer with the Lord.

Now is the time to go back to some of those techniques of Catholic "speed dating" and use them in a much more reflective manner. Pray together. Pray a novena to the Holy Spirit for wisdom, courage, and discernment, or a novena to St. Joseph and the Blessed Virgin Mary, about your call to the vocation of marriage. Pray before the Blessed Sacrament together. Take this very important decision to the Lord Himself, and place the issue before Him, together. Get some spiritual direction together. A relationship with a priest will be very beneficial now. Go on a retreat together for the sole purpose of discerning the vocation of marriage together. Perhaps in the midst of this, a fast from each other is also in order.

Ultimately, the two of you, your own mini faith community, must come back together to answer the ultimate question: are we called together to the sacrament of marriage? Since you each hold 50 percent of the discernment, this is a mutual selection process. There has to be mutuality of assent to getting married; you can't make someone want to marry you. As this is communal discernment, there has to be unanimity if the community—the two of you—is going to go forward.

There are five possible answers to the question "Are we called to the vocation of marriage together": we don't know yet, not now, no and no, yes and no, and yes and yes.

We Don't Know. If the conclusion you both reach is that you can't reach a conclusion, the next steps are easy. You just keep on going. Unless there is some compelling reason to make a more permanent decision (like someone is moving away, or your ages suggest a decision one way or the other needs to be made so that time is not wasted), then you just keep on dating, enjoying each other's company, gathering more raw material for discernment, and keeping your hearts open to the movements of God on this issue. If you don't have the requisite degree of certitude (to a moral certainty) one way or the other, that is a sure indication to do nothing. Maintain the status quo; keep things just as they are. There is no rush. You have not found your "exclamation" yet, each in the other. That does not mean you will not. Keep on living and learning and loving each other, and God will see to it that both of you reach a point of certitude about any call He has for you.

Not Now. What if the conclusion is that you both feel you probably are called but the time is not right, so "not now"? Usually this happens when there is some problem with the circumstances, or insufficient data has been collected, or not enough time or experiences have passed to give one or both partners the certitude they need to get to "yes." Maybe you need to date for a longer time and allow yourself to collect more information. Maybe you need to date others too, to really see what a good thing you have together. Maybe your lives are just in a state right now that makes marriage not what is in order at the moment. Usually "not now" is not about a lack of feeling or regard between you; it is usually driven by some outside situation. If your heart feels right with the person but your discernment just does not take you to "yes" at this time, you still have discerned the vocation together. The experience is not wasted; you two together might build on this in the future.

The conclusion "not now" is usually one that both partners reach; both feel the call to be together, but both somehow have a sense that the timing is off in some way. This situation is a lot like "we don't know." You either keep on dating, or you might break up for purposes of each getting those life circumstances into a better order to eliminate the interference they have been causing. Maybe the feeling is "not now" because you are both still in school. Maybe it's "not now" because one of you has financial troubles. Maybe it's "not now" because one of you has important family obligations. Those are all good reasons to discern that the timing to enter into the vocation of marriage is not right at this point. You want to be open to the timing working out at a later point, all the while being respectful of each partner being free to do what they have to do, and explore other relationships as necessary.

You particularly need to be open to the answer being "not now" if one of you feels quite certain that you are called to marriage together and the other disagrees. (See "yes and no" below.) If God has sent someone into your life who is very convinced you are called together, and you have heard all of his or her reasons for discerning that conclusion, and you can't find any real flaw in their discernment process, you had best be very circumspect that this just might not be the right time for the two of you.

When you are balancing one partner saying "we are called" and the other saying "I am not sure," you need to keep the door open, and keep your hearts open, because this could well be a situation in which the time is just not ripe for the two of you somehow. If after a prayerful and heartfelt discernment one of you feels called, you should not just give in to that discernment over your own discernment of being unsure. But again, you need to keep an open heart and keep on discerning (whether you stay together or separate).

No and No. What if the answer is "no"? The answer is really "no" only if you both agree that it is no, we are not called, and you are both sure of it to a moral certainty. There is no shame in that. You know, everyone you date will end up as a "no" until the person comes along who is the "yes." That you did all the work, went through this whole process with someone, but then you both concluded that you are not called, does not mean this time was wasted. Quite to the contrary. You know what to do now. It will help you discern more and better with someone else in the future. But what you need to do with this person is clear: it is time to break up.

You might be the kind of person who can be friends with a person you have dated seriously. This is a great thing, if you both can do it. Not everyone can. You will know what is right to do in your situation.

Even if you both get to "no," there is usually one person or the other that is more upset about the conclusion. That usually has to do with past hurts, life circumstances, and personalities. Perhaps being friends after dating is not something your partner can do now. That's all right too. If you cared enough about this person to seriously consider marrying them, then you want what is best for them now too, don't you? So the two of you can decide how to handle things after you break up.

Yes and No. The most difficult conclusion of this communal discernment process is if one of you concludes "yes" and one of you concludes "no," each having certitude to a moral certainty. That is a very confusing conclusion. How can that be? You are both prayerful, you are both seeking, you have both gone through this whole process, and you reach diametrically opposite conclusions? One discerns you should enter into the sacrament of marriage and the other discerns we are not called to that at all? How can that be?

Here is the thing: there is only one will of God. His will is totally consistent; He has only one whole big plan. He doesn't have one will for this person, and one for that person, and the two cannot exist along side each other. No, God has one perfect will. So in discerning His will for the two of you concerning the call to marriage, if one concludes "yes" and the other "no," one thing is for sure—God's will is consistent, so one of you is not correct somehow. That is a hard thing to say, but there is only one will of God. He would not call you to marriage with someone and not call them too.

How can you equate this? It could be that one of you just does not have enough data, that raw material of discernment, to discern properly. There is nothing wrong with their discernment itself, just that it's not based on enough data.

Here's an example. Say a man has always held the preference or feeling that he would marry a blonde. The woman he is dating is not a blonde. So his discernment is that she is not his wife. There is nothing wrong with his discernment— he has used the raw material of discernment (feelings and preferences) and judged it, and draws the conclusion that the woman can't be called to be his wife. There is nothing inherently wrong with that discernment itself, but there is something wrong with his data sampling. That is an extreme example, and we all would criticize an important decision being made on this alone as foolhardy, but you get the idea. It could be that one of you just does not have enough data.

Maybe there is data that one of you is ignoring for some reason. "Facts do not cease to exist just because they have been ignored" (Aldous Huxley). While that may be the case, gently try to remove the scales from your partner's eyes, but you really can't make someone see something the person doesn't want to see, if his or her heart is hardened to it at this point. That is God's job, not yours.

If you are the one saying "yes," you can advocate that you two continue on in knowing each other so that your partner can gather more data. This might be a possibility, if you can do it, knowing that at this point he or she doesn't feel called to be with you in marriage, and you do. That might be hard to do, but perhaps you are someone who can do that and not have it do violence to your spirit. One thing you don't do is go into that never-ending dating limbo where you want to get married and your partner doesn't, and that situation goes on for years on end. If you have done the communal discernment, and you still decide to date, set a reasonable time limit to it—how long you will wait for him or her to gather more data and discern more and better about you.

It could be that the partner who discerns "no" is just not hearing God's voice or seeing His hand in the right manner, or is misinterpreting somehow. It is not malicious; they are just mistaken. If there are errors in their discernment, you can lovingly point them out, not subjectively but objectively, and ask that they talk to their priest about what you have observed. This kind of situation is best left for the person to work out with a spiritual advisor, and not with you. You will be seen as someone who is biased, who wants to convince them that their discernment is "wrong" because you want to see the situation conclude differently, i.e., you want to get married. Since you have this vested interest, your point of view can't really be trusted by your partner, not because you are not trustworthy but because his or her heart will only be illuminated to the truth (if that is the case) by God, and perhaps it will be through the wise counsel of a spiritual director that it will happen.

It may be that your partner has all the information, but his or her heart is hardened for some reason, by past hurts, mistrust, life distractions. That is the kind of work that can only be attended to by the Holy Spirit. Someone who is hurt, doubtful, or depressed in general, or going through difficult life circumstances, is going to be hard-pressed to find their "exclamation" about anything, and certainly will have a hard time seeing straight about the vocation of marriage during such a time. You can gently ask them to continue to pray about it, and say that you will continue to pray for them, that God leads them in His will for their life. But when it comes down to it, this is a situation where you are not going to be the source of their re-discerning to another conclusion, that is, the conclusion you have reached. You can't convince someone about discernment. That is something that God has to do, or he will send someone or something to do that. It might be in spiritual direction over time that they see that they were wrong somehow. It might be in an experience, perhaps in another relationship after you, that they see that they mis-discerned about you. Let God work that out, and you just keep on praying, if you really believe you are called together.

It may also be that you both have discerned, and your partner's discernment really points to you, but he is simply exercising his free will to say "no" to you, God's gift to him, and therefore chooses to say "no" to God as well. God gives us each free will, and He can shout the truth at each of us, but we have to respond to that truth. Maybe he does see that you are called, but for earthly reasons does not want to choose you. Maybe he is shallow, maybe he is judging you on earthly values like looks or money, or maybe she wants to keep her options open and does not really care at this point what God is calling you two to do. That is the most difficult situation. All you can do is pray that over time God gives your partner the grace to see what you see.

The tendency is to assume that the person who is concluding "yes" is the one who is correctly discerning and the one who says "no" is the one who is wrong. That might not be the case. It could be that person who is coming up with the "yes" just wants this situation to work out so badly that they are imagining things, such that they are unknowingly letting Satan influence them into thinking that you two are called together. If you think that the partner who thinks you are called is the one who has mis-discerned, all of the same suggestions apply: with great care, point out possible holes in their discernment. Send them to spiritual direction. They might hear this better from their priest than from you at this point. Pray for them, that God enlighten them so they can go on and have the happy life God has planned for them.

If one of you says "yes" and the other says "no," you both owe a great responsibility to the other. If you are the one who thinks the relationship should end, you need to be open to the fact that you could be saying "no" to the greatest gift God will ever send you. Are you really ready to accept the magnitude of making such an error? Also, you owe a great responsibility to the other person to give him or her all the information or answers that they need to be able to go on without you. After all, they have discerned that you are their spouse, the mother or father of their children, the fulfillment of their vocation. Imagine how devastating it is for them to hear from you that you have discerned differently, and the future they saw with you is now disappearing before their eyes. If you cared enough for them to discern the vocation of marriage with them, give them whatever it is they need now so they can go on after this devastating conclusion to your relationship.

If you are the person saying yes, the one having your heart broken at the moment, you have a responsibility as well. Give this person you love so much their freedom. Let them go. Don't try to talk them into something they don't discern at this point. If God has really called you both together, as you have discerned, He will try to change your partner's heart over time. You can't do the convincing. You can't drag someone into the vocation of marriage with you. You don't want that in any event. You want someone who picks you, and only you, and if your partner has doubts, if he does not see what you see, then it's up to God to work out the situation.

A real faith crisis can develop if you have done all this work to discern the will of God, done everything right, and then you find that your partner has reached the opposite conclusion. This can cause a major crisis of faith. If I can't discern this most important question in my life correctly, what good is any of my faith? What am I even doing here, anyway?

The thing to remember here is that everything that happens to you is God's will. There is God's absolute will, what He actually intends, and there is His permissive will, that which He allows to be so, although He is not the source of it. If you find yourself on the receiving end of this kind of devastating conclusion to your communal discernment, know that God has permitted it to be so. So even in this midst of your heartache, know that God is allowing it, permitting it, for a reason you don't understand just yet. Perhaps in time you will.

It could be that over time, God will show you that your own discernment was faulty somewhere along the line. Maybe He will reveal "the tail of the snake" in something you were really depending on as coming from Him in your discernment. Maybe shortly after your communal discernment, something will happen which you never expected that tells you your discernment had not accounted for this unexpected event, and that your partner was right—you were not called together, you just didn't have all the information yet (maybe they had some insight about it that you didn't). Maybe it will be in a life commitment that makes marriage not advisable for you in the near future. Maybe it will be in another love.

Or it could be that your partner is the one who has misdiscerned. Time will tell which it is. But in the interim, you can't convince him or her, so after you have explained everything, it is best to leave him or her to God.

Don't ever forget that discernment is ongoing. There is an endpoint in discerning the call to marriage and that is when you say, "I do." Then the discernment about whom to marry is over. But up until that time, you should still have an open heart to hearing God's call for your life.

If the communal conclusion was "not now," "no," or "yes and no," via good fruits and consolations, bad fruits and desolations, you will soon start to have more certitude, or more doubt, about the discernment you have made together. In these situations, there is nothing like no longer having the person in your life to tell you whether you made a good call or a bad call.

St. Ignatius says that the best test of your discernment is action. If your discernment is that you are not called to marriage, then act on that. Break up, and see what God sends you. Are good fruits and consolations the result, and are they enduring over time? Then you can be more assured that you have chosen wisely. But if things go the other way, and you experience bad fruits and desolations, or if one of you continues to believe that you are called together still, be open to re-discerning the situation as time goes by.

Yes and Yes. To get to a mutual "yes," both of you, knowing everything about your own discernment and about the other's discernment, must believe to a moral certainty that God has called you together to the sacrament of marriage. If you know this in your hearts, you each have just found your "exclamation" in the other. What a glorious conclusion to this process! You both know what to do now. This is one of the most exciting moments in life, realizing that you love a person, they love you, and that you are going to move forward in a life together. Congratulations, and may God bless you both abundantly in your life together. It is now that you make the ultimate exercise of your free wills and say "yes" to each other, make life decisions, get engaged, tell others of your plans, start in with Engaged Encounter and Pre-Cana, and start planning your life together in the sacrament of marriage.

Dietrich von Hildebrand states quite beautifully the mission you have found together: "You have been chosen and called, therefore, as husbands and wives to be for one another the living experiential sign and expression of God's love by sharing with each other the gifts of uncompromising love, unconditional acceptance, ceaseless dedication, total fidelity, and untiring service. These are the signs of God's love, and this is what makes God present in the Sacrament of Matrimony" (von Hildebrand, pp. xxi-xxii).

Conclusion. Always remember that in valid communal discernment, there has to be unanimity. You both have to agree for the "community" to go forward, acting on the will of God. You must have the same will, and that must be the same as God's will. "The chief effect of love is to unite the hearts of those who love each other so that they have the same will" (Jean Baptiste Saint-Jure, *Trustful Surrender to Divine Providence*, p. 37). If you have both prayerfully gone through this discernment process, it is hoped that you reach the same conclusion. If you do, there is reason to rejoice. It means there is going to be a wedding, or it means you are both going to move on to find the persons that God has waiting for you elsewhere, but buoyed along by having met this wonderful person along your path to marriage. Both are things to celebrate.

If your discernment does not agree, there can be no positive movement forward together, but you will have learned a lot from each other, about yourselves, and about the sacrament and the call to marriage, whatever the outcome.

Chapter 13

The Exclamation Revisited

You started this journey searching for your "exclamation," your joyful knowing, of the person with whom God intends for you to serve Him in the vocation of marriage. You started out with the preliminary question of whether you are called by God to the married state of life. You used the discernment process that the Church has employed for centuries to reveal God's will as to whether you are called to the vocation of marriage in general. As part of that process, you have studied God's Word and the Church's teachings on marriage and the moral principles that govern that holy sacrament. You have used all the tools of discernment, gathering and then "sifting apart" your feelings, preferences, conscience, answers to prayer, your reason, the circumstances, signs, consolations, desolations, good and bad fruits, all the while looking for your "exclamation," the recognition of God's spouse for you.

You have honored your God-given gift of sexuality and honored its dignity in the process of seeking a spouse. You have taken the time and put in the effort that an issue as serious as marriage requires. You have asked yourself and your boyfriend or girlfriend some really hard questions, and have had some difficult and intimate discussions. You searched the quiet corners of your own heart seeking God's will concerning your spouse, and you searched the heart of your partner as well.

Maybe you will use this process only once, or maybe you will use it many times on your path to marriage. Either way, it is hoped that at some point, as Adam did, you can say, you can exclaim, "This at last is bone of my bones, and flesh of my flesh." If you can, you have found your "exclamation." You have found the person that God has called you to share with in the vocation and sacrament of marriage. Like Adam, you *know* in the core of who you are that this is the helpmate suitable for you. You might have known right away, or early on, and used this process to confirm what your heart was telling you from the start. Or God may have used this process to reveal to you what you didn't fully see at first. How and when God revealed His will to you for the selection of your spouse is less important than the fact that you are open, seeking, listening to Him, and noting His movements in your heart.

You have just discerned on one of the greatest decisions you will ever make. Whether the answer was "yes," you are called together in marriage, or "no," that there is still someone else coming for you, you have just taken part in a very important exercise of your free will.

The journey is often as important and meaningful as the destination itself. May God bless you and your future spouse, whoever he or she may be.

Chapter 14

A Treasury of Prayers for Use in the Discernment of Marriage

This is a collection of prayers that can be used while you seek your vocation in marriage. Some are written with one gender or the other in mind, but the reader is encouraged to adapt the prayers to their own situation.

Prayer for My Future Husband

Lord, bless my future husband,
    wherever he is today on his journey to me.
Today give him the strength to move one day closer to me.
    Don't let him lose heart, but rather know deeply
    that my heart waits for him alone.
Today let him not be tormented by temptation
    or the near occasion of sin
    that might keep him from the rightful role
    You have ordained for him.
Today, make his work fruitful and his yoke easy,
    so that he is not distracted
    from this highest calling You have for his life.
Today, give him the necessary experiences
    that will ready him to be my true partner,
    the spiritual head of our household,

and the loving father to any children
with whom You may bless us.
Today may his family and friends support him
in his current station in life,
and encourage him as he seeks me.
Today, if it be Your will, intersect the lines of our two lives,
Which in Your divine plan You have drawn so perfectly.
Lord, bless my future husband,
wherever he is today on his journey to me. Amen.

(By the author)

Prayer for a Spouse

Lord, You said that it is not good for us to be alone. You made us for each other. But Lord, I find it so hard to find that mate who would be a good spouse. Help me, Lord, to put this yearning for marriage in its proper place. Lead me, Lord, to the one whom you choose for my spouse. While I wait for You to reveal Your will in this matter, help me to know myself better. Help me to address those areas of my life which are disordered and which would interfere with my having a successful marriage. When my desire to find a spouse becomes all consuming, help me to relax and practice patience. Help me to invest in wholesome friendships which bring me closer to You and which will assist me in making such an important decision. It is so natural, Lord, to seek love. Teach me to seek You first and to learn to give love before I try to receive it. Help me to remember that whatever journey this life leads me on, You are always present, always offering companionship, and always filling my deepest need. I offer You, Lord, my loneliness and my longing for marriage. I wait for You to lead me to Your prefect Will for me in this and all things. Amen.

(Author unknown)

Prayer for a Spouse

All Good Lord, I know that my happiness depends on this, that I love You with all my heart and all my soul, and fulfill your Holy Will in all things. May You Yourself guide my soul, O my God, and fill my heart; I desire to please You alone, for You are my Creator and my God. Preserve me from pride and self love, let reason, modesty and chastity adorn me. Idleness offends You and engenders vice; give me then a desire for diligence and bless my labors. In as much as Your law commands men to live in honorable matrimony, so bring me, O Holy Father, to this calling which You have consecrated, not for the satisfaction of my desires, but unto the fulfillment of Your holy purpose. For You have said, it is not good for man to be alone, and having made woman for a helpmate for him, thou didst bless them to be fruitful, and multiply and replenish the earth.

Hear my humble prayer sent up to You from the depths of my heart: give me a spouse, honorable and pious, that together with him/her in love and accord we may glorify You, the compassionate God, Father, Son and Holy Spirit, now and forever, and unto all ages. Amen.

> (Author unknown; adapted from a
> Russian Orthodox prayer book)

Prayer for the Love of My Life

Lord, I know that I can talk to you, I know that I can trust you in big things, and small things, because you are my Lord.

I want to ask you today something very special. I want to lay in Your hands the person whom I will be in love with one day, whom I will share my entire life with.

I want you to bless her, help her, and take care of her.

Wherever she is, bless her way, lift her spirit, guide her steps, strengthen her heart, show her Your mercy.

Do not permit that anything damages her capacity to love. Even if I don't know this person yet, fill her with joy, make her generous.

Help me, make me dignified to be at her side, Lord, and when we live together may we have a real marriage, may we be husband and wife in Your name.

Wherever she is, bless her, fill her with love and finally, help me find her. Amen.

(Author unknown)

Prayer for the Intercession of St. Peter Canisius
(Patron Saint of Unrequited Love)

Lord Jesus Christ, You gave Saint Peter a vision of Your Sacred Heart. He felt great sadness as he realized that You suffer when we despise, ignore and reject Your love. From then on, he offered up all his work as a sacrifice of devotion to Your Sacred Heart. I ask him to pray for me when my love for another person is misunderstood or rejected. I ask him to pray for everyone who has experienced unrequited love. O passionate Lord, help us to continue giving love no matter how long we have to wait for it to be accepted. Heal our broken hearts with a stronger touch of Your love. Saint Peter, pray for us. Amen.

(by Terry Ann Modica, *Daily Prayers with the Saints for the New Millennium*, Riehle Foundation, 1999)

Prayer to Saint Raphael

O Raphael, lead us towards those we are waiting for, those who are waiting for us! Raphael, Angel of happy meetings, lead us by the hand toward those we are looking for! May all our movements, all their movements, be guided by your light and transfigured by your joy.

Angel guide of Tobias, lay the request we now address to you at the feet of Him on whose unveiled face you are privileged to gaze. Lonely and tired, crushed by the separations and sorrows of earth, we feel the need of calling to you and of pleading for the protection of your wings, so that we may not be as strangers in the province of joy, all ignorant of the concerns of our country.

Remember the weak, you who are strong—you whose home lies beyond the region of thunder, in a land that is always peaceful, always serene, and bright with the resplendent glory of God. Amen.

(From the AveMariaSingles.com Web site)

Prayer for the Fulfillment of the Call to Marriage

Most gracious Father, I come before you desiring a spouse with whom I may live out the sacred covenant of marriage. A spouse who will be my helpmate and friend; a supportive companion on our journey to Your heavenly kingdom. A spouse who will rejoice with me in accepting children as the richest blessing You bestow upon husband and wife and who will share with me the joy of rearing them in the ways of faith. I pray for a spouse to whom I may entrust the deepest longings of my heart; who will accompany me through life's good times and bad, its pleasures and pains, its joys and its sorrows, in sickness and in health, until that day we reach Your kingdom where every tear will be wiped away and we shall see You, our God, as You are, and praise You forever.

Heavenly Father, as I ask that Your holy will be accomplished in my life, I am also confident that my desire to embrace the holy vocation of marriage will be brought to completion and that someday I will marry the person You have chosen for me. Grant me the grace of discernment so that impatience or despair may not obstruct Your plan. I trust the Holy Spirit to lead me and guide me so that when the hour comes, I may know that my choice and Yours are the same. For I know that it is only in doing Your Will that I will find my true happiness and peace. I ask this through Our Lord, Jesus Christ, Your Son, who lives and reigns with You and the Holy Spirit, one God forever and ever. Amen.

(Author unknown)

Appendix

The following is an excerpt from the text of St. Ignatius's *Spiritual Exercises*, specifically, the *Rules For The Same Effect With Greater Discernment Of Spirits*. It is these rules that form the basis of discernment of the movements on the soul, those consolations and desolations, that must be tested to determine what is God's will. It is a good exercise to read this great saint's own words, and you are greatly encouraged to read the entirety of the *Spiritual Exercises* as you continue with discernment for your life.

First Rule. The first: It is proper to God and to His Angels in their movements to give true spiritual gladness and joy, taking away all sadness and disturbance which the enemy brings on. Of this latter it is proper to fight against the spiritual gladness and consolation, bringing apparent reasons, subtleties and continual fallacies.

Second Rule. The second: It belongs to God our Lord to give consolation to the soul without preceding cause, for it is the property of the Creator to enter, go out and cause movements in the soul, bringing it all into love of His Divine Majesty. I say without cause: without any previous sense or knowledge of any object through which such consolation would come, through one's acts of understanding and will.

Third Rule. The third: With cause, as well the good Angel as the bad can console the soul, for contrary ends: the good Angel for the profit of the soul, that it may grow and rise from good to better, and the evil Angel, for the contrary, and later on to draw it to his damnable intention and wickedness.

Fourth Rule. The fourth: It is proper to the evil Angel, who forms himself under the appearance of an angel of light, to enter with the devout soul and go out with himself: that is to say, to bring good and holy thoughts, conformable to such just soul, and then little by little he aims at coming out drawing the soul to his covert deceits and perverse intentions.

Fifth Rule. The fifth: We ought to note well the course of the thoughts, and if the beginning, middle and end is all good, inclined to all good, it is a sign of the good Angel; but if in the course of the thoughts which he brings it ends in something bad, of a distracting tendency, or less good than what the soul had previously proposed to do, or if it weakens it or disquiets or disturbs the soul, taking away its peace, tranquility and quiet, which it had before, it is a clear sign that it proceeds from the evil spirit, enemy of our profit and eternal salvation.

Sixth Rule. The sixth: When the enemy of human nature has been perceived and known by his serpent's tail and the bad end to which he leads on, it helps the person who was tempted by him, to look immediately at the course of the good thoughts which he brought him at their beginning, and how little by little he aimed at making him descend from the spiritual sweetness and joy in which he was, so far as to bring him to his depraved intention; in order that with this experience, known and noted, the person may be able to guard for the future against his usual deceits.

Seventh Rule. The seventh: In those who go on from good to better, the good Angel touches such soul sweetly, lightly and gently, like a drop of water which enters into a sponge; and the evil touches it sharply and with noise and disquiet, as when the drop of water falls on the stone. And the above-said spirits touch in a contrary way those who go on from bad to worse.

The reason of this is that the disposition of the soul is contrary or like to the said Angels. Because, when it is contrary, they enter perceptibly with clatter and noise; and when it is like, they enter with silence as into their own home, through the open door.

Eighth Rule. The eighth: When the consolation is without cause, although there be no deceit in it, as being of God our Lord alone, as was said; still the spiritual person to whom God gives such consolation, ought, with much vigilance and attention, to look at and distinguish the time itself of such actual consolation from the following, in which the soul remains warm and favored with the favor and remnants of the consolation past; for often in this second time, through one's own course of habits and the consequences of the concepts and judgments, or through the good spirit or through the bad, he forms various resolutions and opinions which are not given immediately by God our Lord, and therefore they have need to be very well examined before entire credit is given them, or they are put into effect.

Bibliography and Resources

Church and Papal Documents

Catechism of the Catholic Church (Complete and updated). Doubleday, 1997.

John Paul II, Pope. *Familiaris Consortio: The Role of the Christian Family in the Modern World*. St. Paul Books & Media, 1981.

____. *Original Unity of Man and Woman, Catechesis of the Book of Genesis*. St. Paul Books & Media, 1980. (Preliminary publication to the collection that became *The Theology of the Body*)

____. *The Theology of the Body*. Pauline Books & Media, 1997.

Paul VI, Pope. *Humanae Vitae: On Human Life*. St. Paul Books & Media, 1968.

Pius XI, Pope. *Casti Connubii: On Christian Marriage*. 1930.

Other Books

Cantalamessa, Raniero, O.F.M. *Virginity: A Positive Approach to Celibacy for the Sake of the Kingdom of God*. Alba House, 1995. (Beautifully written homage to the charism of virginity)

Finn, Thomas, and Donna Finn. *Intimate Bedfellows: Love, Sex and the Catholic Church*. Pauline Books & Media, 1993. (Excellent treatment of premarital sex, contraception, and NFP)

Green, Thomas H., S.J. *Weeds Among the Wheat—Discernment: Where Prayer and Action Meet*. Ave Maria Press, 1984. (A must-read book for anyone who is serious about discerning God's will)

Groeschel, Benedict J., C.F.R. *The Courage to Be Chaste.* Paulist Press, 1985. (By well-known Franciscan priest on EWTN; contains excellent list of suggested readings)

Guillet, Jacques, S.J. *Discernment of Spirits.* Collegeville, Minnesota: The Liturgical Press, 1970. (Classic Catholic book on discernment)

Ignatius of Loyola. *The Spiritual Exercises.* Translated from the autograph by Elder Mullan, S.J. 1909. (The foundation of Catholic teaching on discernment)

Kippley, J. and Kippley, S. *The Art of Natural Family Planning.* Couple to Couple League, 1984. (Comprehensive discussion of NFP)

Lawler, Rev. Ronald, O.F.M. *Catholic Sexual Ethics.* Our Sunday Visitor Publishing, 1998. (Scholarly yet readable work on the Church's teaching on sexuality in all states of life: married, single, and celibate)

Merton, Thomas. *The Seven Storey Mountain.* Harcourt, 1999.

Most, William J., S.J. *Discernment of Spirits* (Available in EWTN's online document library at www.ewtn.com)

Plus, Raoul, S.J. *Christ in the Home.* Frederic Bustet Co., Inc., 1951. (How to set up a Christ-based marriage and family, lived with traditional Catholic values)

Provan, Charles D. *The Bible and Birth Control.* Zimmer Printing, 1989. (Outstanding detailed review of the biblical support for the prohibition on contraception)

Sheen, Bishop Fulton J. *Three to Get Married.* Scepter Publishers, 1996. (Classic book by one of America's best-loved bishops)

Trobisch, Walter. *I Married You.* Harper & Row, 1971. (Protestant pastor's wisdom for finding the divine purpose in sex and marriage)

Trobisch, Walter. *I Loved a Girl.* Harper & Row, 1965. (Protestant pastor's letters to a young African couple on sex and marriage) von Hildebrand, Dietrich. *Purity: The Mystery of Christian Sexuality.* Franciscan University Press, 1970.

von Hildebrand, Dietrich. *Marriage: The Mystery of Faithful Love.* Sophia Institute Press, 1984.

Walsh, Msgr. Vincent. *Love and Responsibility: A Simplified Version.* Key of David Publishing, 2001.

West, Christopher. *Good News About Sex and Marriage: Answers to Your Honest Questions About Catholic Teaching.* Servant Publications, 2000.

____. *Theology of the Body Explained.* Pauline Books & Media, 2003.

Wojtyla, Karol. *Love and Responsibility*, Translated by H. T. Willetts. Ignatius Press, 1981.

Other Resources

The Couple to Couple League
P.O. Box 111184
Cincinnati, Ohio 45211
800-745-8252
www.ccli.org

Pope John Paul II Institute for Studies on
   Marriage and Family
415 Michigan Ave., N.E.
Washington, D.C. 20017
202-526-3799
www.johnpaulii.edu

Web Sites

Eternal World Television Network
www.ewtn.com
(Excellent "Question and Answer" section where questions from readers/viewers are posted and answered, including

issues of sexuality, marriage, and NFP. There is also a documents library with excellent source materials under the topic of "Marriage.")

Love and Responsibility Foundation
www.catholicculture. com
(Web site devoted to John Paul II's book *Love and Responsibility*, with summaries from discussion group meetings on the Holy Father's book)

www.singleness.com
(A Protestant Web site about the single life, including chastity, with a wonderful collection of past articles)

Articles

Berchmans, Brother John. *Catholic Marriage.* (available online at www.catholicism.org/pages/marriage.htm)
Herbst, Winfrid, S.D.S. *Kissing and Catholic Morality.*
Kreeft, Peter. *Discernment.* (available online at www.peter kreeft.com/topics/discernment.htm)

Printed in the United States
48927LVS00002B/120